BAD KARMA:
The True Story of a Mexico Trip from Hell

Reader's Favorite 2020

Silver Award Winner!

"Paul Wilson has written a totally engrossing memoir with Bad Karma. His (mis)adventures are incredibly well depicted, as are his travel companions and others he meets along the way—including a guy named Joaquín 'El Chapo' Guzman."

Discovery

Must read!

"So painfully true you wish it was fiction! A laugh-out-loud (to keep from crying) romp about what not to do bridging the gap into adulthood."

The Prairies Book Reviews

"Accessible, crisp prose and a deeply-intriguing account have the reader turning pages non-stop.

Booksiren

"Wilson adeptly explores the generosity, honor, family ties, and faith of the average Mexican. An adventure story and journey of personal discovery at once, this is a must read."

Elizabeth Howard

"Bad Karma has instantly joined the pantheon of great adventure writing!"

Neil P. Reed

"Fear and LOATHING goes to Mexico!"

Kathleen S. Gray

"Exhilarating, Raw, PURE … A story we all wish we'd lived through!"

Karen Ehrlich

"This was a massively entertaining read! I could barely put it down!"

James Q. Benners

"I felt like a fourth passenger on the trip experiencing all the ups and downs that they did. It was an easy thrilling read, well written and I highly recommend this!"

Launa Brockman

"Deftly written and incredibly entertaining! A "laugh out loud" adventure tale. I highly recommend it. Get ready for a wild ride!"

Kirkus Reviews

"A lively and enthusiastic account, this fun read captures a bygone age."

BAD KARMA

THE TRUE STORY OF A MEXICO TRIP FROM HELL

PAUL WILSON

ISBN: 978-0-578-57910-8 (hardcover)
ISBN: 978-0-578-57906-1 (paperback)
ISBN: 978-0-578-57908-5 (ebook)

Edited by Barbara Noe Kennedy
Cover design by Derek Murphy
Interior design by Jake Muelle

badkarmabook.com

DEDICATION

For my grandchildren:

Emily, Clark, Grant, Ford, and Madilynn.

*(Read it when you're old enough … and then
do everything the opposite.)*

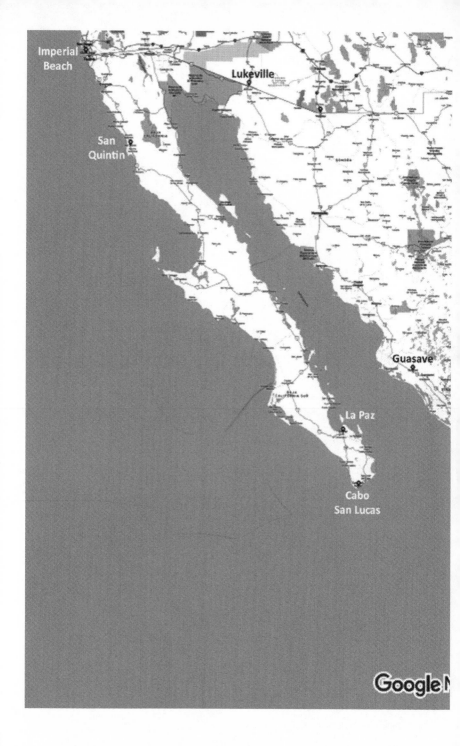

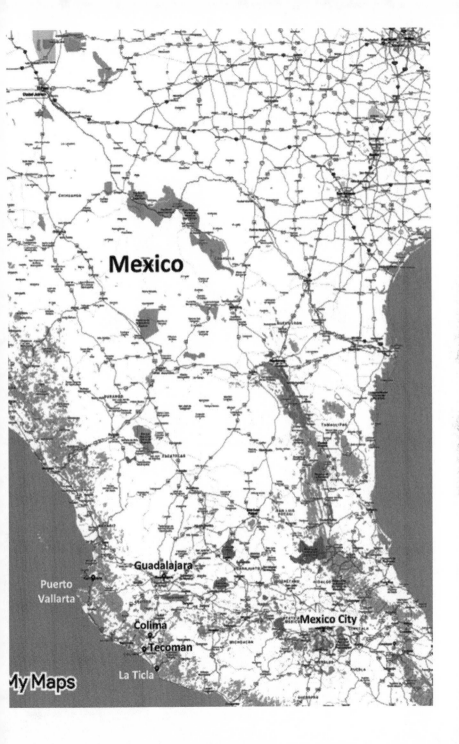

CONTENTS

AUTHOR'S NOTE

This is a true story. All events are as they happened, and the characters are real. I recognized it at the time—*something* incredible was taking place—and this *something* presaged a supernatural purpose. In the space of five and a half weeks, "just wanting to fit in" evolved into having beers with El Chapo. I kept records, notes, and photographs, but was afraid to share much until the various statutes of limitations had expired. A wife and two impressionable children came along in the interim—and this story remained hidden away, lest they discover what a shit I'd been in my twenties. Meanwhile, the legacy of our misdeeds overtook us each in turn, and one by one, *those* scores were settled.

Buckle up and hang on. You'll be "riding shotgun."

CHAPTER 1

NINETEEN SURFERS.
FOURTEEN APARTMENTS.
ONE OLD BUILDING AT THE BEACH

"Heartbreak Hotel," "The Crib," "Stud Estates" aka "The Manor"

It sucks being a wannabe; forever on the outside, looking in. I grew up an introverted nerd (even my teachers called me "Poindexter") and was desperate to escape the cruelty of my self-inflicted social sequestration. No amount of alcohol, drugs, or profanity seemed to crack the mystery of the "cool quotient." Even now, despite being a fixture in "The Manor" the last two years and investing endless hours in the surf every day, I still was considered more of a hanger-on than a resident. Truly earning your bona fides—and being accepted as belonging in the building—was reserved for those who had surfed Mexico. Baja didn't qualify. I'm talking *Mainland*, the farther south the better. There were two classes of residents: Those who had surfed mainland Mexico, and those who wanted to. It was the surf culture's version of sporting a letterman's jacket on campus. People looked up to them. Paddling out with one was akin to an apprentice shadowing a journeyman. In the surfer's pecking order, known as the "line up," the rest of us deferred prime position to them. They got all the best waves—and all the cutest girls. Man, they were cool. I wanted to be "in" in the worst way, and I figured *this* was my ticket.

Over the past few days, a tangible buzz had energized the building. "Moose" and "Jelly" were preparing for a trip to the mainland. Yeah, we all had nicknames. Not like "Moon Doggie" or "Gidget." Those are lame. Our names were cool … except maybe for mine. Early on, I was tagged with "Paul E. Opters," and it stuck. I suspect it was because I was seen as "helicoptering around" the upper-tier residents too often to be cool. Still, it was better than my neighbor's moniker. The morning he was christened "Stinky Feet," his given name, "John," was retired forever.

Moose had been to the mainland. Hell, he'd been everywhere. He was so cool, he'd even been in jail a few times; mostly drug stuff, as far as I knew. Jelly hadn't been. To the mainland, I mean; not jail. Even so, he must have earned his credentials some other way. Perhaps it was the overly confident façade, or the string of beautiful girls' broken hearts he trailed. Either way, Jelly qualified as a "big man on campus," too.

They were each a few years older than my twenty-one. Moose was a master manipulator; I'm guessing it was his idea, and I was roped in from the beginning. They let me overhear them planning their trip, knowing I'd do just about anything to be included. Turns out, neither of them had a vehicle that would make the trip. (I learned later, they'd tried the same ruse on everyone else in The Manor who owned a vehicle that would suffice, and I literally was the last viable option in the building.) They played me like pros. I assured them my 1966 VW Bus was perfect for the trip. It had a killer stereo with six speakers, twin amplifiers, and a subwoofer powerful enough to make silverware dance on the flip-up table that held my stove. I'd harvested the chilly-bin portion of an old mini-fridge and modified it as a hidden icebox under the custom-made full-size bed. My Bus was so cool, it even had a name and custom license plate: 1DRBUS, aka "The Wonderbus." Too naive to realize I was being used as a convenient tool, I laid it on thick—a car salesman, hungry to make quota, couldn't have been more persuasive, nor been more stoked when the sale was closed. *Not only was I being included on the trip, it was* my *Bus that was making it possible! If this didn't garner me top-tier status, it was beyond my reach.*

A few not-so-minor details of the trip began to filter out. It was to be a two-month surfin' safari, plunging nearly two thousand miles into the rugged, coastal jungles of southern Mexico. I had a full-time job (and nowhere near the cash to cover such a trek), but backing out now would be coolicide. And that's what gave rise to a Saturday night just like every other Saturday night.

Only completely fucking different.

May I have your order, please?

I'd convinced my best friend, "Perro," to be an accomplice. (Spanish for "dog," his nickname had morphed over the years from "Horn-dog." How he'd earned it, I'll leave to your imagination.) He and I had been sworn enemies in middle school, where I was a year ahead of him by virtue of skipping the third grade. We met in first-period Woodshop. I was an eighth grader and the "shop aide" (read: "insufferable teacher's pet"), and Perro was the consummate class clown. It was my job to make sure all of the hand tools were put away, machines cleaned of sawdust, and floors swept at the end of class—and it was left to me to assign those chores to the seventh graders. I took woodshop so seriously, I was an aide for first-period Beginning Shop, had Intermediate Woodshop for second period, and Advanced Woodshop for sixth period.

Up until that point, I'd little to no experience being in charge of anything, and Perro—boasting a lifelong track record of being a little shit—made my life miserable. I'd assign cleanup of the table saw to him and return to find its cutting surface newly elbow deep in sawdust, scrap, and cuttings, Perro sitting on top, cocking his index finger behind his thumb and placekicking one nugget at a time through some makeshift goalposts. *Nothing* could get him to take things seriously. That all changed one day in 1969, though, when he overheard me grousing to another classmate that we were too poor to own a television, and I was going to have to watch the moon landing at a neighbor's.

Perro got up in my face and let me have it. "Hey! What do you know about being poor? Your family lives in those apartments with the pool, and you're complaining about not having a TV? The whole time I was growing up, we lived in tents and moved all the time. My family went out and picked fruit every day. I thought we were camping! It wasn't until last year my mom told me we were transient farmworkers when I was a kid. So shut the hell up! You have it made!"

It was at that moment Perro and I became blood brothers. I finally understood why he was so happy and carefree about everything. To him, he was living the dream: A house he could call home; parents he was fiercely proud of for what they'd accomplished; and friendships he was now safe to make, knowing they wouldn't be cut short by the end of yet another harvest season.

Since then, we'd experienced a multitude of things together, but had our own unique perspectives on most everything growing up. He held his own with three older brothers who pummeled him frequently; and I had three sisters I wasn't allowed to hit back. He was half a foot shorter than me when we met, but he shot up past me in high school before I passed him back the summer after graduation. He lived in the same house and school district for years. My family routinely wore the awkward badge of being evicted for nonpayment of rent and lived in eight different school districts during that same time. I became the one who couldn't count on a friendship lasting beyond our next move. So, when it came time to try and pull off something that might prove to be life changing, Perro would be my partner in crime. I wanted to surf the mainland, and this was how I was going to get the cash: I would steal it. But not directly. That would've called for far bigger cojones than mine.

I ran the nightly restock crew, did some of the ordering, and had keys to the front door of a busy supermarket in Coronado "Island," the next town north. Coronado isn't an actual island—though the residents snobbishly consider themselves a prime-rib community. It's bordered by water on three sides, and the Navy's SEAL Team One base provides a formidable buffer from the hamburger hamlet of Imperial Beach to the south. (Even the federal government plays along, calling the navy base in Coronado, "North *Island* Naval Air Station.") In my store, clearly the nicer of the two supermarkets in town, the aisles always were abuzz with activity, whether customers during the open hours or the restock crew at night. That is, except for three hours once each week, when it was stone-cold empty from 12:01 a.m. to 3 a.m. Sunday morning, when I showed up to let in the crew.

I'd worked out every detail and rehearsed it in my head a hundred times. The plan was to enter the store a little after midnight and have everything I intended to snag, sitting on the edge of the rear loading dock by 12:45. From there, Perro would dump it all into the back of his truck, and then drive the twelve miles south to our apartment. I figured I'd be there to help him carry the spoils up to our second-floor apartment and still have plenty of time to get back to the store to open up for the crew by 3.

I'd let my fellow Manorites know I'd be doing some "after-hours shopping," and a steady parade of orders rolled in. To my surprise, even a couple of their moms stopped by with lists. (No wonder the building was chock-full of miscreant ne'er-do-wells!) I asked what they'd like, and we negotiated a price. An accidental stroke of genius, I was killing two birds with one stone: getting supplies for the trip, and financing my part of it.

The stockroom was always a mess. No one even noticed the pile I'd accumulated behind a bunch of back-to-school crap. I'd carefully engineered two pallet loads to resemble useless overstock by stacking cases around their perimeter—leaving a large void in the center of each where I could toss the smaller prizes helter-skelter. Four cycles of "over-ordering" provided ample cartons of products with which to construct the pallet walls, their foundations laid with 30 cases (that's 2,160 cans!) of Chicken of the Sea "packed in oil" tuna (more than 1,400 of which were for Stinky Feet's mom! In retrospect, I suspect she was filling orders for her friends as well. *No one* likes fish that much, do they?); 10 cases (240 jars!) of Jif Extra Crunchy Peanut Butter; enough Folgers Coffee to open a bistro—and beer. I wouldn't be cool without snagging some beer ... well, not just *some* beer, a *lot* of beer. In fact, it worked out to be one pallet of everything else—and one pallet of beer. I'd "shopped" during my regular shifts, depositing a can of this or package of that, until both pallets (and my neighbors' preorders) had been filled.

Give me a sign

12:35 a.m. I'm alone in the store, heart pounding out of my chest, my mouth so dry I fear I'll choke on my tongue, charging down the aisles, pushing one basket and pulling another, scooping up stuff like a contestant on Supermarket Sweep. Why the panic? Once word of what I'd planned made the full circuit around The Manor, a flood of last-minute must-haves poured in for a bewildering mishmash of things.

Could it be I'd oversold what I could deliver? Oh man! I was going to be soooo cool! ... *But only if I didn't let anyone down.*

I have to kick it up a notch. My list is long and I'm determined to fill it. Razors, batteries, sunscreen, a meat thermometer, beer, beef jerky, film, party napkins, candy, cigarette lighters, a dozen canned hams, more beer. ... I pile everything on top of the two already overloaded pallets, grab the pallet jack handle, and muscle the first ridiculously heavy and teetering load to the roll-up door. 12:42. *Good. Three minutes early! I should wait to open the door. Don't mess with the plan.* I double-check the time. Still 12:42. An alligator drop of sweat splats across my watch. Shimmering beads of perspiration trace my feet on the stockroom floor. *How can my mouth be so dry and my skin so wet? Damn, it's quiet. I don't remember the fluorescent lights humming before.* Check my watch again. 12:43. *You've got to be kidding me. One minute? One lousy minute? What am I thinking? This whole stunt is nuts. Actually, it's not too late to wise up. I haven't broken any laws yet, have I? What a drag to get caught. But a bigger drag to put all this crap back! And the cool factor. The Mex trip. I gotta do it; and do it now before I lose my nerve.* Time? 12:44. *Screw the time, I'm raising the door.*

Perro sits behind the wheel of his pickup truck parked across the street, precisely according to plan. No turning back now. I drag the first pallet, spin it 180 degrees, and maneuver it into place—partially overhanging the edge of the loading dock—before squeezing the pallet jack handle as gently and precisely as I can, releasing its hydraulic fluid with a muted squeal, and easing it down. It'll be easier to dump its load into Perro's truck that way. Part of the pallet unsupported, its wood creaks, pops, and groans under the load, threatening to fail. The clattering of the pallet jack, as I yank it free, screams through the still night air. There's a row of tidy little, white clapboard beach cottages across the street. Someone's bound to complain. Six days a week they have to listen to this racket, and I'm ripping 'em off of their one night of peace. I spin the jack into position and ram it home under the second pallet. *Wham! Wham! Wham! Wham!* There's just no quiet way to do it. *How ironic will it be to get busted on a disturbing the peace call?* This one's mostly beer. *Is the law harsher for stealing beer than it is for canned tuna and peanut butter?* Again, the pallet's so heavy it's lurching and weaving like it'd flunk a field sobriety test. *Easy does it.* I pivot the load a little too quickly and panic-scramble around the left side to keep an ominously leaning wall of beer from falling. *God, my hands are shaking!* I withdraw the jack and flash a thumbs-up to Perro. He nods and drops a left-handed salute in return. I lower and latch the door. 12:50. Five more minutes, and Perro will have our booty on the road. It's *my* plan, and it's working perfectly.

Something doesn't feel right as I lock the front door of the dimly lit supermarket and cross the empty parking lot. My part done, I was to leave the store, head back to our apartment, and wait for Perro. But something is off. I can taste it. Rather than drive off right away, I sit in the 1DRBUS, staring at the store, and fumbling with my keys, consumed by indecision. My formerly white T-shirt, now translucent and pasted to my chest with sweat, revealed my surfer's tan. I'd drilled Perro too many times to count. *"Stay with the plan, don't change a thing."* *Was I above my own rule? Since it was my plan, wasn't it also my call to stray from it now? Was I just freaking out, or was this a moment of clarity?* 1:02. Twelve minutes now since I'd signaled Perro and lowered the roll-up door. He should be on his way south with the load by now. *Would it hurt to double-check?* It was totally against the plan—but I couldn't *not* do it. I *had* to check on Perro.

Out of the lot; into the street; turn the corner and … *I can't freakin' believe my eyes!* His truck hasn't moved from across the street! Our two pallets of loot sit untouched, spotlighted by the loading dock lights like the stars in a *Broadway freakin' musical!* Panicked, I pull alongside Perro. He's loaded, alright! Face into his shoulder, arm draped out the window, out cold! He hadn't signaled me at all! I'd watched him pass out!

Perro!!!

PERRO!!!!!

GODDAMMIT PERRO!!!

He snorts and awakens with a start. His eyes drift gradually back into alignment. "Wha …? It's okay, I'm awake! Oh fuck! Look at all that shit!"

I'm practically apoplectic. We're fifteen minutes late already. The plan is out the window.

"Get everything into your truck as fast as you can! I'll go around the block and check for cops. I'll be back in a couple minutes and follow you home."

The neighborhood around the store is deserted tonight. No cars. No cops. No one at all. There must be something going on across town. *This is much too quiet. So be it. Maybe karma is smiling upon us after all,* I think as I pull back around to check on Perro again.

Holy shit! I've badly overestimated how much will fit into the bed of his truck! He's in the loading bay alongside his truck, floundering shin-deep in cans and packages, working to keep even more of them from spilling over the side—and losing the battle. *How'd I fuck this up? Do cases of stuff expand when they're dumped into a truck and not stacked? Did I forget to allow for the wheel wells?* The heap mimics the silhouette of a camel and dwarfs the eight-foot bed of his truck; it's twin humps soaring two feet higher than the cab!

Perro spots me, just as a sixty-four-ounce can of Hawaiian Punch tumbles free and bangs loudly off the side of his truck on its way to the pavement.

"GODDAMMIT, Opters! How the fuck am I supposed to fit all this shit in my truck?" he demands in a drunkenly loud voice.

I sound hoarse and struggle to muster a loud whisper. Throat so dry, I gag on my words, unable to complete a sentence without forcing a swallow every few syllables. "Fuck that! … We're way late! … C'mon…! We gotta go…!"

Hansel and Gretel

Perro fires up his truck and eases it slowly up and out of the loading area. A heavy-duty, full-size, three-quarter-ton, lifted, four-wheel-drive, Ford F-250XL pickup truck; it's odd to see it so obviously overloaded and canted rearward. Reaching ground level, Perro rolls the truck gingerly over the little hump where ramp meets sidewalk. Despite the abundance of caution, a baker's dozen cans and several jars of peanut butter break loose, tumble down from the Himalayanesque load, and crash to the ground. The sound is that of a baseball bat whacking a piñata filled with Mason jars. Perro slows to a crawl, looks back at me wide-eyed, and shakes his head.

Too rattled to think it's funny, I mouth a silent, "Go! Go! Go!" in return.

We are such a bust.

Not only do we have a truck piled high with stolen beer and groceries, we're littering and disturbing the peace. All this, as we drive through Coronado, California—possibly the most uptight coastal town in the country—at 1:20 a.m., on a Saturday night in the summertime. A staunchly conservative community, the city combats crime and homelessness by promptly driving any sketchy characters over the eleven-thousand-foot *San Diego–Coronado Bay Bridge* and depositing them, now safely out of their sight, in downtown San Diego. Coronado routinely leads the nation in traffic citations and DUI arrests per capita. They don't have use for pink-flamingo yard ornaments. On any given night, cops have people standing on one leg all over town, and the lawn jockeys may as well be offering up a pair of handcuffs.

Perro must be sobering up. He's following the route through town I worked out to avoid the main streets—and hopefully the cops. It's a backstreet that cuts straight across the island, but everyone hates it because of the ridiculously exaggerated dips at each intersection.

Oops.

Possibly underestimating the weight of the load, or forgetting just how severe these dips are, Perro roller-coasters through the first intersection. A split second after the truck bottoms out, thousands of cans, jars, and packages levitate in unison. Up and over the two-lane hump. Repeat. *Oh, the humanity!* Cans and jars bail overboard from three sides, skipping and skittering wildly in every direction. A canned ham cannonballs into a parked car, leaving behind a crisp horseshoe-shape imprint on the driver's door; a gooey sneeze of ham juice graces its window. Obscene smears of broken-glass-festooned peanut butter trail the truck. A school of tuna cans machinegun a trio of shiny metal trash cans curbside.

Across the street, a car alarm's flashing lights and blaring horn heralds our passing. Beers are bursting everywhere in my path—geysers of yellow suds fill the air, conjuring visions of being shelled by some unseen prohibitionist. My windshield wipers on now, the air reeks of a bad frat party.

With a newfound respect for the dips, Perro slows to walking speed through the next eight or ten intersections. Nevertheless, the load continues to shiver and nest, in a packaged-goods game of musical chairs. Nonconforming cans and jars continue their migration toward the sides of the truck's bed, only to plunge as lemmings to their death. We're almost through town and make the turn past the Navy's S.E.A.L. Team One Training Base. At last we can accelerate to highway speed. We pass the base's main gate guard shack. Right on cue, the flap on a twelve pack of beers, perched atop the tailgate, pops open, and a volley of cans drops in sequence, like depth charges rolling off the stern of a destroyer hunting an enemy submarine. I watch one of the military sentries point us out to the other.

WE ARE SUCH A BUST!

The next five or six miles take us along the narrow isthmus of sand that separates San Diego's bay from the Pacific Ocean. It's a dark and desolate stretch, and the police have better things to do on a Saturday night than patrol it. Temporarily free of immediate peril, I notice Perro's right taillight is out. *Un-freakin'-believable.* Another sixty-four-ounce can of Hawaiian Punch leaves his truck and bangs hard against the underside of the 1DRBUS, the sharp blow resonating into my feet. Surely by now, someone is hot on the trail of groceries and beer we've left in our wake. Every ruptured can-splat on the pavement paints an unmistakable arrow to the scene of the crime. We're a modern-day Hansel and Gretel, leading anyone who cares to notice, right to our door. At minimum, they'll know we left town headed south toward Imperial Beach, because we're marking our route along the only road that goes there. Worse, there's not another car on the road to dilute the odds of our being identified as the perps.

Sacrificial van

One more bend in the road, less than a mile to go. *I can't believe we're going to get away with this!* Perro drifts onto the shoulder for a few seconds before he catches himself and corrects. The minor swerve kicks up a cloud of dust and sends another medley of merchandise over the side, further reducing our bounty. Something catches my eye in the darkness up ahead; I strain to make it out. *SHIT! It's a Coronado Police car!* In two years, I've *never* seen a patrol car tucked into that spot at night! Daytime, yes. It's a notorious hiding place for a speed-trap cop during the day. *But now?* I spy his little red radar-gun light pointing at us as we pass, and quickly check our speed. Fifty-eight miles an hour. *Good.*

Oh shit! His lights just came on and he's pulling onto the highway behind me. *Shit! Shit! Shit! Shit! Shit!* He closes to within a couple of car lengths behind me. I don't think Perro's even noticed him yet. *I have to think. I don't want to go to jail. I can't go to jail! What was I thinking!? This was so stupid! Okay, gotta think. ... I have an idea. If I crash, he'll have to stop and see if I'm okay, and Perro can escape home. What if Perro doesn't realize I've crashed on purpose, and he stops, too? That would suck. Sacrifice myself for Perro, and have it be for nothing. I gotta do it. We can't both go down. I'd rather go to the hospital than to jail. ... I think. Yes. That's it. I'll veer off to the right if the cop makes a move on us. I wonder if he'll think I've been drinking. My van reeks of beer. I'll bet he can smell it from where he is. There's no way he's not going to pull me over.*

13

Another quarter mile and we'll be out of Coronado. *FUCK!* His reds and blues just came on! I take a deep breath and brace for the impending crash. The cruiser whips around to my left so fast I lose sight of him for a split-second, and hesitate. He's by me in a blur, accelerating up the passing lane toward Perro.

Did I just chicken out? Everything's happening so fast, I'm confused for a second. *Okay, I can still crash when he pulls in behind Perro. He'll have to stop ... right? I mean, he wouldn't just leave burning wreckage in his rearview mirror to pursue some guy littering ... would he?*

Once more, I gird myself for impact. *One, two, thr... Wait!* He just blew past Perro, too!!! The cop streaks up the road another hundred yards, whips a U-turn, and zooms off northbound—siren on, reds and blues strobing all the while. He's responding to a call from back in Coronado!

Oh my God! I wonder if he got summoned to go investigate a bunch of cans in the road? I think I just wet my pants. Who would notice? I'm soaked in sweat, but breathing. The gods are smiling. We've made it back to our own neighborhood.

They call our town, Imperial Beach, a quaint little coastal cul-de-sac, officially famous for being the "Most Southwesterly City in the Continental United States." Big-Freakin'-Deal. IB's true claim to fame is as the original "Meth Capital of the U.S." We referred to it with mock affection as, "Venereal Beach, Where the Debris Meets the Sea." Our cops were Barney Fyfe clones; Hells Angels the authority figures.

We were home free.

CHAPTER 2

READY ... SET ...

Over prepared

I was never in the Boy Scouts. My dad said it interfered with the hours I was expected to work at his speaker cabinet business. I did spend a couple of years as a Cub Scout, and would've done just about anything to participate in Little League Baseball, but once I hit nine years old, my dad had had enough of me frittering away my time. After school and weekends were for work. I'd earned ten cents an hour until I was twelve years old, and then got double that 'til I was almost fifteen. I was always paid "On Account" (on account of he didn't have the money). My mom kept the ledger up to date. My dad couldn't be bothered with such things himself, and I don't believe he trusted me to keep it myself. I'd check my balance every week, thinking I was gonna see that money someday. I suppose just believing I had money "On Account" somewhere made me feel pretty good.

One June afternoon, when I was about eleven years old, I accidently banged up my dad's car while horsing around with my then, best friend, Charlie Brown. (He's dead now. Heroin.

But yep, that really was his name.) In that instant, my ledger balance went from $94.30 to minus $5.20. (Do the math. That's just shy of *one thousand hours* I'd logged from ages nine to eleven. I had to work fifty-two hours just to get back to *zero*.)

My dad had a favorite stick that he used to stir paint and mix resin with. Over the years, it had acquired a hard, thick coating composed of layer upon layer of dried material. What started off as a half-inch-square-by-eighteen-inch-length of hardwood was now round and the diameter of a baseball bat handle. My backside was not wholly unfamiliar with it. Even trivial offenses such as neglecting a chore or asking him for something a second time, when he'd already said "no," inevitably earned a whack or two. Even so, that afternoon I overheard my mom on the telephone, tearfully pleading with my dad to calm down before she went to pick him up, obviously afraid of what he might unleash upon me. When the call was over, she told me he'd promised not to hit me, but insisted she bring me along, ostensibly for a good chewing out.

He was waiting for us, resin-coated stick in hand, when we pulled up. My mom got between him and me and begged, "Jack! You promised not to hit him!"

He pushed her aside. "I'm only going to give him a small sample of what he *should* be getting," and proceeded to tee off on my butt and the backs of my legs until he was too tired to go on.

I missed school for a few days, unable to walk more than a couple of steps; my blue jeans sticking to the blistered skin. Sitting was out of the question. My flesh bore an angry weave of purple, red, and black interlaced welts from the top of my ass crack to the backs of my knees. Enough? Not with *my* dad. He put me on three months "restriction," too. Now I know restriction to a lot of kids translated to "No riding your bike" or "No television." Heck, I would've killed to have a bike or a TV to be restricted *from*. My family had been restricted from those luxuries for as long as I could remember. Nope. Restricted wasn't a "take something away" proposition to my dad. It was an "All you're gonna do is work for me this summer" kind of deal.

And that's exactly what I did. Since I had to ride to and from his shop with him, I was trapped; forced to work the same hours he did. While everyone I knew was gloriously free of school, out building forts, chasing rabbits, or playing at the beach, I cut insulation, sorted and bagged hardware, scooped sawdust, and painted cabinet backs. The only time he spoke was to tell me what to do next. Ten hours a day, six days a week. (Thankfully, my mom hauled me to church on Sundays, in spite of my dad, an avowed atheist.)

He was an asshole in every way, but I did learn *one* important thing from watching him run his business—and that brings me back to the Boy Scouts. I knew how to prepare. My dad had drilled into me: Being prepared was *more* than being ready for the things you expect to happen. To him, worry and negativity were the paradigms from which one truly practiced readiness. The axiom, "Expect the best, but prepare for the worst," wasn't lost on my dad. Except to him, having the worst happen—*and* being prepared for it—was the pinnacle for which one should strive.

It was three days 'til were leaving for Mex, and I was at least marginally aware that I'd succumbed to the fallacy of covering every possible need for our trip down south. Still, I compulsively prepared for any conceivable calamity.

Let's see ... two thousand miles each way, another thousand miles of random exploring, dusty conditions ... a case of motor oil ought to do it. Hmmm ... I own an extra carburetor, better bring it. Extra fuel pump, distributor ... you never know. Spark plugs, points, condenser, coil? No brainer there. Pack 'em.

I had a freakin' VW parts store on board. To me, packing is an art form. I'd grown up putting my dad's shit away every day, and now I stocked shelves for a living. Packing is like a puzzle: a place for every piece, and every piece in its place.

Moose and Jelly each accountable for their own stuff, I assumed the responsibility for the "shared" necessities fell to me. Besides, it was *my* vehicle, and I couldn't expect anyone but me to think of everything we might need. Moose and Jelly held the mindset that, a single, shared bar of Ivory soap could serve as shampoo, laundry detergent, dish soap, you name it. *Amateurs.* Me? I had trial-size packages of everything, from aspirin to toothpaste—a hundred miniature trophies from my after-hours shopping spree—shaving cream, body wash, shampoo, conditioner, Band-Aids, and sewing kits. *A dozen of each ought to do it.* I had snacks and lunches more than covered: Eight dozen food bars, reams of beef jerky, a case of peanut butter, and canned tuna out the ass.

Man, Moose and Jelly are gonna think I'm so great!

Anything, I mean freakin' anything, we could want or need for this trek … I had us covered, and then some.

Surrogate dad

I figured we were short a cooler. Even though the 1DRBUS had a built-in icebox, we'd surely need a second "chilly-bin" solely dedicated to beer, right? There was no question of who to ask to borrow one from. In our neighborhood, when something was needed you didn't already own, you could always rely upon the "full-service" garage of Racoo's dad.

Mr. Recker was an engineer or something, and along with Mrs. Recker and "Nanna" (Racoo's grandmother), the Recker clan lived in a spacious, ranch-style home on the beach directly across the street from The Manor. Mr. Recker was cool. In fact,

I held the fanciful notion he secretly wished *I* were one of his kids, too. Not that Racoo was a bad guy or anything, just not what you'd think of as ambitious. Racoo: smoked pot, surfed, smoked pot, ate, smoked pot, played his guitar, smoked pot, took naps. ... He had it made. His room was beachfront; bed positioned so he needed only open his eyes to check the surf. Mrs. Recker prepared his meals, washed his clothes, made his bed. ... A regular "Harriet Nelson," she was.

Racoo and the family puppy, "Max"
sharing a plate of spaghetti.

Now that I think about it, the thing between Mr. Recker and me probably went both ways. I would have taken him over my dad in a heartbeat. Not for the beachfront, responsibility-free crash pad; although that'd work just fine. ... No, Mr. Recker treated me like I had *value*. He wanted me to do well in life. He lived life according to the principle, "There's plenty of pie to go around," and believed—seeking abundance for everyone—ultimately paid off more handsomely than hoarding for one's own benefit, without concern over who might be getting a leg up on him. His "success philosophy" was at once difficult to place all of your stock in, and impossible to dismiss.

One afternoon, Mr. Recker was putzing around in his garage and called out for me to come over.

"Hey Paul."

"Hello, Mr. Recker."

"Paul, I saw you and some of the guys headin' off with golf clubs the other day. Do you play much?"

"No, I'm just learning. We went to a little pitch-and-putt. It's fun. I think I'm getting the hang of it."

"Do you have your own clubs?"

"We only needed a sand wedge and a putter. Little Ricky let me share his clubs, but he says I need to get my own if I want to go with him again." (Rick had stopped growing at just over five feet and despised being called "Little Ricky," but Mr. Recker knew the little sniveler by that name, rather than "Tampon Taylor," the nickname *we* all used for him.)

He listened intently. I had the sense he was mulling something over. Not waiting for me to finish, he raised his hand, index finger extended in a "shush," and signaled me to stay put for a moment. Pulling keys from his pocket, he put the "hold" sign up a second time with his free hand and wrapped around to the rear of his car, popped the trunk, and hefted his golf bag from its regular spot.

"Paul, I'm planning on buying myself a new set of clubs this weekend. Do you think, if the price was right, you might like these old ones?"

He played golf several times a week and owned a *beautiful* set of clubs (expensive ones). I knew deep down he'd much rather be passing these on to Racoo. Unfortunately for Mr. Recker, his son spent his days surfing, smoking pot, playing his guitar, and napping, leaving precious little time for golf.

"Wow, Mr. Recker! You serious?" I caught myself. "Uhh ... errr ... well ... uhh ... how much were you thinking of asking for them?"

Surely he'd seen the enthusiasm drain from my face, before opening with, "Well, I paid four hundred dollars for the set a couple of years ago, and I figure they should still be worth about half of that."

Before I could interject, he continued, "Thing is ... I really don't want to give up my lucky putter here." With exaggerated reverence, he lifted a well-worn putter from the bag and set it aside. "But, I think I could let the rest of the set go for, say ... How's twenty bucks sound?"

I bought the clubs. Mr. Recker held them a week until I had handed over the second of two ten-dollar payments stipulated by our handshake-sealed agreement. Upon delivery, I spent the whole afternoon cleaning and polishing. From there on out, when they weren't in use, the clubs occupied their own special corner of honor in my bedroom. After the 1DRBUS, those golf clubs were probably the most treasured thing I could call my own. So, when I went looking to borrow an extra cooler for the trip, I started the mission in Mr. Recker's garage. True to form, he insisted that I take his "go-to," red-and-white, all-steel Coleman ice chest, a couple of lanterns, and the family's set of camp cookware as well.

Looks don't count

Barry was a vagabond surfer from New Zealand who'd recently latched onto The Manor. I don't think anyone had ever actually invited him to hang out, but he'd made himself at home on one couch or another for weeks. Maybe it was because his Goldilocks' blond hair, boyish good looks, and distinctive "down under" accent brought the girls around—and, they typically traveled in pairs. It was easy to tolerate a guy who always showed up with an extra girl. I know *I* bought beers for four, more than once. It's a wonder there weren't more "Barrys" around. *What a cool gig!*

I liked Barry 'cause he had a '66 VW Bus like mine. Well, "like mine" in the most general sense. Mine could've rolled off a showroom floor. Barry's carried the look of a salvage project reclaimed from the local junkyard. The 1DRBUS had: custom paint, chromed bumpers, matching curtains, wood-veneered interior, full-size bed, built-in icebox, foldout stove, a kick-ass stereo. … Barry's bus didn't even have a passenger seat.

Life isn't fair; I couldn't help thinking whenever Barry would show up with a couple of hot chicks sitting among the rags and fast-food wrappers in the back of his bus. Hell, I could barely get a girl to stick her head in my window to take a peek. But *this* afternoon had a whole different air about it. My back was straight and my chest puffed, for today I was somebody to envy. We were leaving for the mainland in the morning! Every square inch of the 1DRBUS sparkled like a jewel in the sun as I finished up a final coat of Turtle Wax and Armor All. In the midst of fogging a stubborn smudge on the front bumper with my breath, Barry rolled his beater bus in alongside mine.

"How's it going, mate?" Barry asked, his attention clearly elsewhere.

"Yo vámonos a México en la mañana para los dos meses." *Hey, might as well show off what little primitive Spanish I can muster.*

Paying little heed, Barry swung open the passenger-side double doors on his bus to reveal, what else? Two cuties, sitting cross-legged in a pile of random debris. I repeated myself to

Barry in plain English, and loud enough to be certain the girls could hear plainly this time just how cool I was.

"Dude … Moose, Jelly, and I are splittin' south in the morning. We're talkin' two months in mainland, mate!"

Not about to divert attention from himself, and already knowing the story, Barry barely flinched. "Right-on, mate. Got any cold ones for my friends here?"

Brushing past him, the hotter of the two girls sidled right up to me and spoke giddily, "Wow! Mainland for two months? Are you excited?"

Ah-hah! I thought to myself smugly. *It's the "adventure" thing that gets the chicks!*

"Yeah. I'm totally stoked." *That's the best I could come up with? Why does my brain go dead around cute girls? She's obviously into me, right? I gotta do something to keep her attention.* I motioned toward the open, passenger-side barn doors of my own bus.

"Look how prepared I am." *No wonder I'm alone. What a dork.*

"Really? Lemme see."

You're kidding. Hey, maybe she has a thing for hapless nerds!

I started to say something else, but she cut me off.

"Where're the beers?"

So that's the ticket. I'm gettin' played. Boy, she and Barry are birds of a feather. I'm not into any of that bullshit right now. My fully laden cooler of iced-down beers is for the trip— not these clowns.

"Actually, I have more gettin' ready to do. You know, … like cleaning my windows and stuff … uh … maybe another time." *That sounded totally lame, but why should I care?*

"Don't fret, mate. We can see you're busy pimping your ride, but …" Barry turned and looked his own piece-of-crap bus up and down, flashed an annoyingly toothy smile at the girls, leaned into me, and in a whisper loud enough for all to hear, "Just remember, mate. … It's not how she *looks,* it's how she *runs* that counts."

The girls accepted Barry's arms and off the trio went, linked at the elbows, in search of a fourth, with beer, to make it a party.

Who's smug now? I've been mooched on enough by Barry and his random floozies.

Besides, I've got work to do.

Left to right: Racoo, Barry, and Racoo's mom, working on Barry's VW Bus. Man, the guy was smooth. He not only rebuilt his engine *in* the Reckers' driveway, *with* the Reckers' tools; he convinced Mrs. Recker to help. I'll bet he became a politician back in New Zealand.

Karma's tipping points – Strike 1: The camera

Like so many sticks of straw on a camel's back, even karma has a point of no return. Pass it, and there's gonna be hell to pay, penalties exacted, pain inflicted. I believe I recognized the tipping point in my own case. I'm not certain Moose or Jelly ever did. Oh sure, they knew some of the things they did were wrong, but dismissed it as "crap they got away with." I don't think either of them ever considered the possibility of God (or the cosmos) keeping score. (Stoned, and feeling philosophical one night, Moose quipped to me that, "Two wrongs were his right, as long as he didn't get caught," and I did nothing to disabuse him of the notion.) The transgression that became *my* personal karmic breaking point, I believe, was *the camera*. In retrospect, it was karma herself, offering me an out at the last moment. One final opportunity for me to do the right thing ... or not.

I didn't know the guy personally. Called himself "Dan-O." Said he was a friend of "Pop-fish," one of the sage patriarchs of The Manor. Dan-O was a heroin addict. A full-blown, "rob his own grandmother to get a fix," scum-of-the-earth addict. And here he was, standing in my apartment, obviously Jonesin', and clutching a grubby knapsack. I could barely understand him. Pure hype-speak. An urgent, "fits-and-starts" stream of consciousness, barely coherent babble, reminiscent of Tom Petty with a buzz on.

"Dude ... I hear you're headin' to Mex. with my bros, man."

Bitchin'. This is the last guy in the world I want knowing I'm gonna be gone for a couple of months! Thanks, Poppy.

"I ... I got a camera, man. Got it in La Jolla yesterday ... I mean ... this morning ... yeah, this morning, man."

He had the shakes, stammering out his words. A clear drop of snot grew under his nose, preparing for launch.

"Check it out, man. Pop-fish says you're into takin' pictures ... you know, man ... he said you ... he said you wanna make a surf movie or something."

Halfheartedly, I started to wave him off, but curiosity slowed me as he plopped his knapsack on the kitchen table. He didn't say a word. I wasn't sure he could; he looked lost.

His hands didn't function in sync with his brain. I noticed he had "bum fingers"—conspicuously sun-darkened skin, and rough, overgrown fingernails—with God-knows-what caked under them. He fought with the zipper. In a single, seamless motion, Dan-O punctuated the struggle, turned his head and wiped his nose on his shoulder, his shirt patently accustomed to the practice. Losing the battle of wits to the zipper, he glared at it in frustration and shoved the pack at me.

"Open it, man ... you'll see ... it's what you ... you'll see ... I got it this morning, man."

I really didn't want to participate in this any longer, and my body language gave me away. His fist drumming the table, Dan-O thumped out an awkward cadence for emphasis, narrowed his eyes, cocked his head just a bit, and leaned in to make his final pitch.

"C'mon man ... I came a long fucking way ... Pop-fish told me ... you gotta help me out here man ... OPEN IT, GODAMMIT!"

He smelled like used motor oil or spilt battery acid or something. *I gotta get him out of here!*

"Take it easy, dude. You want me to check it out? I'll check it out. No worries, alright?"

I tugged the zipper and the bag opened easily, revealing the top half of an expensive leather camera case.

Shit, this looks like a nice one.

Cutting through the stench of Dan-O, I detected the sweet aroma of fine leather, with just a pinch of new metal, a fragrance uniquely familiar.

Standing tall, arms crossed in front of him, Dan-O rocked back on his heels, clearly proud of his merchandise. Like I was unwrapping a birthday gift he picked out especially for me, he softened his tone:

"Open it man ... you'll see. Those ornamental fucks have good shit."

Ohhh man, ... he was offering me some poor Japanese tourist's camera. Not just any camera, either. It was a brand-new, top-of-the-line, Nikon XL8S Super-8 movie camera with power-zoom, telephoto lens, slow-motion, and freeze-frame. ... The same camera I'd drooled over for months!

"They had a tripod too, but I had to drop it, man ... they were chasin' me, man. ... Lil' fuckers almost got me! Dude, think it's true about all those fucks knowing kung fu? They were totally yellin' some shit, man."

I looked up from the camera for a moment and watched my new "friend" gaining a second wind. He was riding an adrenaline rush—reliving the morning's score—and leaned in again to make a point. A renegade snot-drop missed the camera but graced my table.

Bitchin'.

Unfazed, he continued, "Check it out, man. There's ... there's like all these movies in little boxes, man ... right here in the side, man."

This zipper cooperating, Dan-O opened a side compartment and my heart jumped in my throat. Disneyland, Knott's Berry Farm, SeaWorld, Kiko's wedding. ... Right there. Plain as day. Modest red-and-yellow cartons of film lined up in a perfect little row, each one meticulously labeled in crisp, black Magic Marker. No wonder the people were so pissed. It wasn't only their *camera* being ripped off. Cameras can be replaced. Heck, it was probably even insured. It was their *movies.* An epic milestone vacation, and a family wedding—memorialized for all eternity—on film, and stolen by a lowlife, scumbag hype. They had to be devastated. I felt a physical crush of guilt against my chest and unconsciously recoiled from the bag.

"They were fuckin' stupid, man. Left it right there on the front seat, man—where anybody could snag it—just like that [snapping his fingers for emphasis]."

"Gimme two hundred bucks, man. It's worth double that."

This guy has no clue. It goes for $870 at Nelson's Camera downtown ... maybe a thousand with tax, the bag, the extras.

I struggled to maintain an air of indifference, but this camera had everything I'd ever wanted.

"I'll give you seventy-five." *Did I just say that? What the hell am I thinking? I don't want anything to do with this! It's dripping in evil.*

Flashing his drug-withdrawal fed temper again; Dan-O slammed an open right hand to the table and screamed at me, "Fuck you! $125 or I'm out of here!"

"Chill, Dan-O! Don't have a fucking coronary. Lemme have a closer look at it."

Consciously intimidated and struggling not to show it, I slipped my fingers into the camera grip to still my tremors. I brought the viewfinder to my eye and gazed around the room. Dan-O shadowed me as I drew the blinds and power-zoomed in on the Reckers' back patio across the street. A crystal-clear image of Racoo's bullmastiff puppy, Max, obsessively lapping at a grease stain under their BBQ, filled the viewfinder.

Damn, I like this camera! If I don't buy it, someone else will. At least I'll *appreciate it.*

"A hundred bucks, Dan-O?

"All right man. A hundred bucks. It's a deal."

He extended his hand to cement our negotiations with a handshake, and I tepidly obliged.

Now, what have I done? All of my trip money was stashed in the bedroom—and I owe part of it to an avowed thief. Worse yet, one who was standing in my kitchen! Do I ask him to step outside for a minute? Think … what do they do in the movies? Maybe I'll just leave the bedroom door open a crack while I fetch the dough. Yeah, that's it. … It'd be pretty stupid to close the door and leave him out there with all my stuff, right? Mustn't look awkward. Fuck! I wish Perro were here to watch my back!

"Make yourself comfortable. I'll get your money." Sounds like I'm asking him kick back and hang with me. *Geeez. I'm a real "mi casa, su casa" kinda guy, aren't I?*

"That's okay, man. … I gotta be somewhere, … just get my money, man."

I took a couple of steps toward my bedroom, and sensing him behind me, turned and held up the "Stop" sign.

"Look, Dan-O, I said I'll get your money. Wait here a sec." Motioning toward the table, I added, "Just sit over there." *How obvious was that? Well, shit. What does he expect? He knows he's a dirtbag. Would HE want HIM in HIS bedroom?!*

He got the message and stayed put … sort of. He shifted from foot to foot, to and fro like he'd just come in from the cold – or had to pee. I needed to get this over with and get him the fuck outta here. Into my bedroom, I opened the closet and wondered if he heard the door roll aside. I glanced over my shoulder to check. There he stood, harshly backlit in the doorway like an ax murderer in a horror movie.

Oh well, we're leaving in a few hours. I'll find a new hiding place when I get back. Old jacket, unroll the hood, there it is: Seven hundred bucks. *Wish he hadn't seen the whole wad.* Trying to shield his view, I fumbled with the cash a bit. Without thinking, I licked a couple of fingers to make the bills easier to peel off the wad. *There's that smell again. Good God, it's awful!* An all too vivid image of Dan-O's hands and fingers flashed in my head – my stomach lurched. *I have to spit somewhere.* I couldn't help it; I was gonna gag. Wrapping three fingers into the nearest shirtsleeve, I did my best to swab the toxic slime from my tongue.

Dan-O took a step toward me. "What's wrong with you, man? You see a ghost, dude?"

"Nothing, man. I think a bug flew in my mouth. Tastes like shit."

Peeling off five twenties, I tucked the rest of my cash into the small pocket stitched into the side of my boardshorts, pressed the flap closed, and gave it a couple of pats to make damn sure the Velcro was holding firm. A full whiff of "eau de Dan-O" reached me. I swear it was enough to make your eyes water. *DUDE, PLEASE! Get outta my bedroom! I gotta sleep in here!*

"Back to the kitchen. I'll give you your dough."

He retreated from the doorway and felt behind him for the kitchen, never shifting his gaze from the hundred bucks in my hand—the perfect caricature of a dog awaiting his dinner bowl. I pointed to a chair and motioned for him to sit. He dropped on command. *Sit! Stay! Rollover! … Damn coldhearted of me to think that way.*

I fanned the twenties out on the table, not wanting to make contact with him again. Dan-O scooped them up, counted his money out loud, and rose to leave.

"Right on, dude. You scored. I gotta go, man. Pleasure doin' business with you, man. I'll come back and have some beers with you sometime, man. … Later."

Now we're buddies??? Bitchin'.

"Yeah, sure man. Right on."

The front door opened and I received a parting blast of *that smell.* Reflexively, I cupped my mouth and nose in my hand. Oblivious to the unintended affront, he left with a fresh spring in his step.

Back to the kitchen, I used dish soap to wash my hands and face the minute the door closed behind him. I felt like

I needed a shower and a change of clothes, but anything I would consider wearing right then was already packed in the 1DRBUS for the trip. It was just me and my fancy new camera now. The guilt began anew. I couldn't take my eyes off the neat little row of red-and-yellow boxes on my table. With equipment like this, the movies in those boxes *had* to be good. This guy was no slouch.

The cold reality struck me. *What am I going to do with his movies?* My conscience said I couldn't just throw them away. *That's just wrong on so many levels.* These people came halfway around the world to make these movies! *Maybe I should try to find the owner somehow? Naw, that'd be stupid. Just get myself busted. Maybe if I do the deed incrementally, the guilt will let up?* Twisted logic prevailed. Robotically, and one by one, I peeled back the seals and opened each roll to the light, exposing the unprocessed film. You can't see film go bad when light hits it. It just instantly does its thing, and then it's over. I knew this placed me squarely into the same low-life league as Dan-O, but there was no going back. It was done. Now ruined, the film could be thrown away. *After all, it's no good to anyone anymore, right? I felt like shit.*

I gotta put this outta my head, or it's gonna affect my Mex trip.

Karma's tipping points – Strike 2: Manslaughter

I'd just finished heating up some leftover spaghetti, when Perro burst through the front door.

"Moose killed someone last year." He dropped it like a bomb.

"Whaaa?"

"It wasn't like he did it on purpose or anything. But yeah, he killed his girlfriend in a car crash. I just found out. Jelly told me. Opters, you remember when we first moved here and he had his jaw all wired up?"

"Yeah, I knew he'd been in a bad car crash, but ..."

"Well, the rest of the story is he was all fucked up on pills, and ran his car into a tree on Bonita Road. Killed his girlfriend instantly, and fucked up the other two people in the back seat."

"You're shittin' me."

"No man. They found him guilty of manslaughter last month, and he's supposed to report for confinement tomorrow. He's out on bail."

"But, we're leaving for Mex in the morning ..." My mind was a blur. "You mean he's skipping *out?*" My voice cracked like a prepubescent boy's, on "out?"

"Yeah. And *you're* his ride across the border, Paul."

Wow, Perro had used my real name. Nobody ever used real names at The Manor. Not around parents. Not around girlfriends. Not around bosses. This is serious.

Struggling to absorb the situation, I slumped backward into the couch and twiddled the sticky pasta with my fork. "So ... what'd he do again?"

"Moose killed someone and now he's using you to split to Mexico. What part of that don't you understand?"

I went numb. *The Tonight Show* theme was surrealistic coming from the old black and white television in my bedroom. A disjointed collection of thoughts bolted through my mind. I realized I'd been holding my breath for who knows how long. Watching my best friend's eyes for some sort of sign, I waited for something to break the heavy silence.

"That's bullshit, Perro. Why'd they let him stay out of jail all this time?"

"Jelly told me the lawyer got Moose's confinement delayed until the wires came off his jaw and he was eating okay. I'm not shittin' you, Opters. You'd better pray you don't get caught taking Moose across in the morning—or you're going to jail right along with him."

"What should I do?" *Boy, do I sound meek?*

"I don't know. You're fucked whichever way you decide. Moose will fuckin' kill you if you bail out now, and you'll go to jail if you get caught taking him."

Perro wasn't using *"kill"* for its dramatic value. He wasn't too far from reality with his summary of the predicament I was in. Moose had the physique of a linebacker and the disposition of a rabid pit bull. He was the best guy to have in your corner and the absolute worst to be on the outs with. We all tolerated him because his mere presence in the water kept all the other surfers away from "our break." One morning he broke up a statewide surf contest out front by charging and screaming at each of the contestants until they fled the water. One poor soul stood his ground. Moose bear-hugged him, swam to the bottom, and held him there until he nearly drowned. The organizers took down their canopies, packed up their trophies, and *that* was that.

"Goddammit, Perro! If you hadn't told me, I wouldn't have known."

"Stupid is no excuse for the law, Opters. You taught me that. Remember?"

My mind was a jumble and this took a second to interpret. "You mean: Ignorance of the law is no excuse."

"See? I'm right. You're fucked."

I started to explain, "If I hadn't known Moose was breaking the law by riding with me …" With a sigh, I gave up. "You're right. I'm fucked."

Perro extended his right hand, grasped my shoulder, and, with feigned empathy, "Hey, what are friends for? So what're you gonna do?"

The die had been cast. My alternatives were unsavory, yet crystal clear. If I bailed out on Moose and Jelly now, I was fucked—pure and simple: I might as well have started looking for a new place to live. If I gambled sneaking Moose across the border, there was a fifty-fifty chance we made it unnoticed.

"You can't tell *anyone* that I know about Moose, okay? You've gotta promise to keep it quiet."

"So, you're goin'?"

"We leave in the morning."

Satisfied he'd completed his mission, Perro noticed the camera beside me on the couch. I told him about my visit from Dan-O, and it being stolen, but never uttered a word about the discarded film to a soul. I didn't need the extra guilt trip. No, that deed was all my own, and it nagged at my heart as I finished my, now cold, spaghetti.

Paul Wilson

Rummaging through your cupboards and eating your food was a form of bonding for Moose. His family kept a bedroom for him in their home thirty miles east of San Diego, but he embodied the American version of Barry from New Zealand (without the accent and the cute girls). He lived couch to couch and cupboard to cupboard off of just about everyone in The Manor.

CHAPTER 3

... GO

"Hey God"

It was two in the morning and I'd given up on sleeping a couple of hours ago. Guilt and nervous energy fueled a nonstop stream of questions, peppering me relentlessly: *I wondered if the supermarket had figured it out yet? Was there anything I could've done to get that poor guy's film back to him? They wouldn't really put me in jail for taking Moose across the border, would they?*

An irrepressible shudder washed over me, trying to awaken me from this nightmare. Man, I am so out of control right now ... what the fuck was I thinking? Any ONE of those things gets me arrested and screws up my life. I wonder whom exactly it is I'm trying to be like—or be liked by—that has me doing such pathetically foolish things? Moose or Jelly? I don't want to end up like either one of them! I mean, Moose has only two options in his life at this moment. Go to jail, or run from the law. He's like, twenty-five or twenty-six and going nowhere *I'd* envy. And Jelly's phantom plant business won't miss him if he's gone for two months? Not to mention, his Mexican lime-importing scheme, or whatever the next hair-brained idea he's yet to spring on the world will be? He's a twenty-four-year-old, part-time waiter—and that's the highlight! I don't think anyone has a clue how it is he pays the rent each month.

Rolling out of bed, I quietly checked my bedroom door to make sure I'd locked it, then walked to the window and drew the blinds. *I'd be mortified if anyone knew I was about to do this!* Oh, what the hell. Kneeling at my bedside, I stumbled into a beginning with, "Hey God … I mean … Dear God … uh … I've been screwing up a lot lately, and I'm sorry about that … really. I'm not just saying that or anything, okay?" *I don't think this is going too well.* "Uh … I just want you to know that I realize I can't keep doing bad stuff, and that I'm gonna stop before I do something *really* bad, okay?" *I wish He'd help me figure out how to say this to Him better.* "Okay, here's what I'm trying to say … God, if you could please help me stay safe on this trip to Mexico and, uh … come back in one piece … I promise to never do more of the crappy stuff I've been doing lately."

BLAM! BLAM! BLAM!

"Opters! Get your ass out of bed! Time to go!" Moose was at my bedroom door.

My doorknob rattled. "C'mon, Opters! We see your light on. Let's go already!" Jelly was out there, too.

Well, here we go. Oh yeah, … "Amen God."

Opening the door, I feigned a yawn and rubbed my eyes. "Jesus! You guys startled the shit out of me!"

Moose raised his left hand, holding one of those plastic, woven-mesh "shopping bags" Mexican peasants used for everything. It bulged with swim fins, snorkel, mask, boardshorts, and what appeared to be two or three rolls of toilet paper. He was wearing the ragged *huarache* sandals he did everything but surf and sleep in, and a yellowed, threadbare T-shirt identical to the one I'd used to polish my Bus the afternoon before.

"The rest of our shit is down by your van. Lemme have your keys so I can throw this in the back."

The 1DRBUS was perfectly packed. A place for everything, and everything in its place. The last thing I wanted was for anyone to *throw* anything in the back.

"Hey, if we're ready to go, we're ready to go. C'mon, I'll show you guys where to put your shit."

"Whatsamatta Paul E. Opters, don't you trust us?" Jelly asked in butchered Three Stooges' speak.

"Nah, man. Let's just get on with it!"

Evidently, the two of them had been up and busy getting road-ready for a while. Thick black bungee cords anchored their surfboards to the rooftop racks, the rest of their gear lay in two loose groupings near the 1DRBUS' passenger-side barn doors. One pile consisted of what you'd expect of someone heading off to a third-world country for the next two months: sleeping bag, cot, backpack, duffel bag, mask, fins, snorkel; and a spearlike thing with a surgical-tubing loop at one end, called a Hawaiian sling. The other grouping wasn't exactly what anyone would call a "pile." An old blanket rolled and bound with a piece of frayed hemp rope, a tattered brown-paper grocery sack, and a ratty old cardboard box with no top. Before I could guess whose was what, Moose scooped up the bedroll and tucked the old carton under his free arm.

"What's in the box, Moose?"

Jelly chimed in before he could react, "Dirty magazines. Moose says it's Federale insurance, but he really just wants to wank off in your Bus."

"Fuck you, Jelly. I told you about the checkpoints, Opters," said Moose, holding up a thoroughly dog-eared magazine.

"Give the Federales a couple of these and you're their best friend. They can't get ones like these down there. It's against the law to show hair or something … I don't know … I just know they work. Gotten me outta some shit."

I asked the obvious: "If they can't get them down there, doesn't that mean we can get in trouble for having 'em?"

"Yeah probably, but don't worry about it. They're better than cash for bribing the Federales. Trust me."

Yeah, "trust me," coming from the guy who hasn't said anything about using me to run out on jail time tonight. Yeah, I trust you alright.

"Either way, I don't want them out in plain view so fit 'em under the bed somehow, okay?"

Meanwhile, Jelly had finished stowing his gear and climbed into the passenger seat up front.

"Shotgun!"

"Only 'til we get across the border, Jelly!" Moose blurted out, then caught himself mid-thought. "Uh … you … uh … I need to show Opters how to get to the toll road once we get across."

Yeah, right. Wanting to hide out in the back when we cross over has nothing to do with it, does it?

Moose grunted and cussed under his breath, struggling to wedge his carton of smut into the cabinet under the bed. "Goddammit, Opters! You got so much crap under here, there's no way this box is goin' in! What's this fuckin' pipe thing for?"

With an "oomph" and a solid-sounding "thud-wham," he tossed aside the jack, wedged his trove into the opening, and latched the cabinet door.

"That *pipe thing* is our jack, Moose! In case we get a flat or something."

"Fuck it. You worry too much. If you don't bring it, we won't need it. Find another place for it if you're so goddamned committed to having trouble!"

There I stood, cradling the jack in front of me on outstretched hands as if an offering, pondering what Moose has said—and the reality—that there was *absolutely no room* for the jack, unless it was underfoot.

"I'll be right back." For once in my life, I'm gonna expect the best and leave the jack behind.

Stairs, two at a time all the way up; lean the jack against the wall just inside my bedroom door; jump the last three steps on the way back down. I was back at the 1DRBUS in thirty seconds—but not quickly enough. Only Jelly's backside was visible as he leaned into the open driver's-side window of his girlfriend's car across the street.

"What's up with Jelly?" I asked Moose, his elbows on the back of my seat, his big head more than filling my own, driver's-side window.

"Ahh … Sherri's tellin' him he can't go or something."

Coarsely sucking in a breath, he bellowed across the early morning quiet: "C'mon, Jelly! You coming or not?"

Jelly straightened, turned, and spat a response: "Shut up Moose! I gotta deal with something."

Sherri visibly was shattered: Tears rolling down her face, sobbing in heaves, and doing little to conceal it.

"Have some manners, Moose. I mean … goddammit! Sherri looks like she just found out somebody died or something. Cut 'em a fucking break!" I felt a momentary swell of pride for actually standing up to Moose. *Nobody* did that, and didn't pay for it.

Jelly backed away from her window, and I caught the tail end of him quietly saying what sounded like, "Whatever. I gotta go."

"YOU BASTARD!" Sherri screamed, as if just now recognizing a cruel deception or suffering a mortal wound. "YOU PROMISED ME! You bastard, I hope you die down

there! You promised … You promised … you …" Sobbing
overtook her ability to speak coherently and she collapsed
into the steering wheel. "Y … y … y … you … ba … ba …
bastard!"

Having never so much as looked back over his shoulder,
Jelly reached the 1DRBUS and opened the passenger door, his
tone serious and subdued. "C'mon. Let's get the fuck out of
here."

The staccato *pop-pop-pop-pop-pop* of the old Volksy's
engine heralded an eerily befitting curtain fall to the scene as
we slowly accelerated away from The Manor.

$6.66

The border was a ten-minute drive from The Manor. North
for half a mile. Stop. Turn right, and head east for two miles.
Turn onto the freeway and head south for three miles, and
you're in Mexico.

Jelly was locked in a fixed stare, somewhere past the
rearview mirror mounted outside his window. Moose lay on
his stomach lengthwise on the bed, both feet hanging off the
end nearest the front, his head propped in his hands like he's
settled on the living-room floor to watch some television,
engrossed with the neighborhood fading away out the back
window. We were five minutes into the trip, about to hit the
freeway, and no one had spoken a word thus far. Deep in our
own thoughts, I don't think anyone noticed the conspicuous
silence.

"We need to stop at the Speedy Mart and gas up." My
voice sliced through the quietude and, with it, the palpable
tension.

"You're fuckin' kidding. You didn't get gas yet?" Moose
growled into the back window without changing position.

"Don't worry about it. I want to top off with good gas before we cross over. We'll be putting plenty of that PEMEX bullshit through it soon enough. Hey, the market's open. Is there anything else anybody needs?"

"Yeah, right. What're we gonna throw overboard to make room for it?"

Even though he was being a smartass, I'm thinking Moose had a point as I walked inside to prepay the gas.

The place was empty, save for the clerk.

"Pump Three. Here's ten bucks, but it's only gonna take about six to fill it." I said, laying the bill on the counter.

"Headin' to Mex?" I half-recognized the clerk as someone I'd seen in the water. "The two of you look like you're ready for a long one."

"Yeah. There's three of us. One guy's in the back." *Why tell him that? I mean, Moose is hiding in the back so I can sneak him across the border to escape going to jail, and I'm Mr. Full Disclosure here. Too late now, dammit.*

"Cool. Hey, I've seen you and the other guy in the water. That's Jelly, right?"

I nodded and he continued, "Who're you?"

I hated this part. "They call me Opters."

"What?"

"Opters. Paul E. Opters. It's a stupid name, but that's what everyone calls me."

"What's it mean?"

"I don't know. Hey, is that pump ready to go?"

"Yeah, sure." Breaking eye contact, his voice drifted a little, betraying a hint of rejection.

"Have a good trip."

Finally. Poor guy must have been bored to death working this shift, but it wasn't my job to keep him company at three in the morning. I figured I was rid of him and turned for the door.

Just as I pushed, he hit me again. "Hey Opters ... you didn't tell me who the third guy is.

Maybe I know him, too."

All I wanted to do is pay for some gas and get on the road. Who is this guy, the freakin' Commissioner of Information?

"I'll be back for my change in a minute." That'll work for now. If the change isn't too much, I'll just leave it. Nah, it'll be at least three or four bucks. I'll need to think of something to tell him when I go back for the change. One thing's for sure: I can't let on to the other guys the pinch I've gotten myself into.

Two dollars ... three dollars ... four dollars ... That's the way, keep it going! *Never thought I'd be rooting for the gas bill to be as high as possible!* Five dollars ... Six dollars ... The pump missed its cue to click off, and squandered fuel backwashed from the filler and dribbled down the side. The tank wouldn't take another drop. Pump nozzle in my right hand, I reached to flip the "off" lever with my left. I froze at the numbers peeking through the dingy, yellowed plastic window on the pump: $6.66. *There's no way in hell that I'm stopping this sale at $6.66!*

The 1DRBUS had a couple of "pop-out" vent-windows along each side, which opened just a few inches; enough to provide some air for people riding in the back. Sticking my nose into the gap of the one nearest the filler, I asked, "Hey Moose, check and see if the gas cans in there are full."

Moose's thick, stubby-fingered, catcher's mitt of a hand crushed a wad of cloth and brusquely pulled the curtain away, partially tearing it from its mounting. Grunting and groaning (he had a way of making every movement sound like a chore), his face contorted and pulled close enough for his nose to bump the glass. His labored breath fogged the clean window.

"Goddammit, Opters. You know if they're full or not. You packed and unpacked 'em ten fuckin' times today!"

"I need your help for two seconds. See if the cans will take a little more. This fucking pump clicked off at six-sixty-six and I'm not leaving it like that. It's a bad omen. The devil's number."

Moose, obviously losing his patience, bellowed back, "POUR SOME GAS ON THE GODDAMN GROUND IF YOU HAVE TO! LET'S GET THE FUCK ON THE ROAD ALREADY!"

"... ROAD ALREADY! ..." echoed in the cool predawn air. Up to my tiptoes, as tall as I could stretch, I managed to see over the top of my Bus, spying my new friend, the self-appointed "Commissioner of Information"—hands cupped to the window inside to provide a glare-free portal, his vision fixed in our direction. It was time to go.

Two quick clicks of the handle, and ten cents worth of gas sprayed into the pump island's trash can, already brimming with fast-food wrappers and wads of blue paper towels. *I hope the guy inside didn't see me do that.* The pump registered $6.76. Now safe to end the sale, I returned the nozzle to the pump and climbed back behind the wheel. *Fuck the change; we're outta here.*

The engine fired right up and we rolled out across the sidewalk and into the street. Catching some curb, the Bus heeled over in a lurch reminiscent of Perro's overloaded truck not all that many nights ago. No wonder, ... I thought to myself ... half that crap's in here now ... plus the three of us!

Over the line

The posture of the Mexican border-crossing cops always struck me as being very casual. The feeling they evoke was: It isn't all that important who, or what, you were bringing into their country, because once you—or it—was *in* their country, they had *ownership*.

I was concerned this crossing might be different, though. One look at the 1DRBUS, and there was no doubt we were on a serious excursion south. Rooftop surfboard racks stacked. Rear wheels splayed outward, exposing the secret of the obvious overload transported inside. And it hardly took a trained eye to spot the anxiety written all over Jelly's or my face.

I'd never really considered it before, but are the "Border Ahead" highway signs supposed to provide you notice ... or heap anxiety on already nervous wrongdoers?

LAST U.S. EXIT BEFORE INTERNATIONAL BORDER

Our headlights caught the reflective white lettering. Each swimming in a field of midnight blue, the warnings appeared to float toward us in the blackness.

NO FIREARMS ALLOWED IN MEXICO

Taken in series, each sign undeniably meant to up the ante.

INTERNATIONAL BORDER
ALL LANES STOP AHEAD FOR INSPECTION

Yeah, right. It's always been a scene reminiscent of a third-world kaffeeklatsch at the guard shacks. An absent-minded nod. A barely perceptible hand motion to proceed on your way. Was that intentional? Did they hope you stopped and asked them if they're through "inspecting" you? Was it meant to weed out the nervous ones?

ABSOLUTELY NO U-TURNS

With a grunt and an "ooof," Moose relocated himself to the floor behind me.

"Only stop for the guard if he orders you to."

"Whaa …?" I broke it off mid-syllable. Fifty yards to go. No time to protest now.

INTERNATIONAL BORDER
LEAVING U.S. – ENTERING MEXICO

There was almost no one crossing into Mexico at this hour on a Friday morning. The cones had been laid out to merge the four lanes into one. The Policia Fronteriza shack scarcely was larger than a tollbooth, yet two guards—engaged in an animated discussion—inhabited the space. A third officer hung monkey-bars-style from the doorway. This guard loosened his grip, dropped the few inches to the pavement, and stepped into our path as we drew nearer.

"I gotta stop, Moose. The guard is blocking the lane."

I got a whispered, "Shhh!" in return. Maybe I shouldn't have been talking to Moose since he was hoping not to be noticed, eh? Maybe the asshole should've told me I was helping him duck jail—and run off to Mexico—BEFORE we got to the border!

About fifty feet to go, I turned off the headlights. *Anything* to avoid pissing these guys off.

One of the two officers wedged inside the booth was barking something in Spanish to the lone Policia standing in our path. His partner leaned from the shelter and Frisbee'd a clipboard full of paperwork to our guy. Eyes on us, it smacked him squarely in the chest and clattered to the pavement. Papers scattered, triggering laughter from his buddies.

Our guy spun, and in the stillness you clearly could hear him rip into the others:

"¡Cállate! ¡Pinche pendejos!" For dramatic effect, the clipboard and papers remained unretrieved as he stepped from our lane and back to the shack. Giving the finger to the others, he spat, "¡Besen mi culo, ustedes!"

It wasn't readily apparent who was in charge, and the three guards were really going at it now. Being careful to avoid crunching the clipboard with my tires, I kept rolling as the front bumper eclipsed the scattered papers. We were being ignored. Not sure of what should happen next, I peeked over my shoulder and shot a puzzled expression to Moose.

"Go, go, go, go, go!" he whispered, wrist-flicking his pointer finger for emphasis.

Jelly concurred with a flurry of mini-nods one easily could interpret as tremors.

Here goes nothing. Ease off the brake, gently let out the clutch, and quietly motor on by—albeit at less than walking speed. We never fully stopped, just the same. Jelly's and my eyeballs were glued to our respective side mirrors, searching for any indication that we were about to be pursued, but the guards were engrossed in their argument, oblivious to us. Now, a couple of hundred feet into Mexico, it was time to shift the 1DRBUS into second gear. Lights off, we quietly dissolved into Tijuana's early morning darkness.

"What the hell were they saying, Moose?" Jelly made his presence formally known for the first time since leaving The Manor.

"'Shut up you fucking assholes,' and 'You guys can kiss my ass.'" Leave it to Moose to translate Mexican trash-talk verbatim.

Never one to dwell in the past (even when that *past* was three minutes ago), Moose leapt into the here and now with a

"We're gonnne! Turn on your headlights and that kickass stereo of yours, Opters! We're headin' to La Ticla!" Distinctly grunt free, he maneuvered his melon between mine and Jelly's and let rip a stress-cleansing, guttural, "YYEEEEAAAAAHHHH!"

Too mind-fucked to think anymore, I set the volume as loud as it would go and pushed "play"; having already cued up Bruce Springsteen's *Born to Run* before I went to bed last night.

All three of us believed we knew the words, but no version was exactly the same. Unfazed, we belted it out the best we could. The adrenaline rushes and worries of the last few days had weighed heavily upon us, and our minds needed the break. We were responsibility-free kids for the time being, and three shit-eating grins broadcast our collective relief. None of us had a clue—these were destined to be the last, truly carefree moments we would enjoy.

It was probably just as well.

CHAPTER 4

———

PUT ON NOTICE

Frijoles by flashlight

For the next hour and a half, we cruised the toll road south along the Baja Norte coastline. Jelly had grown quiet again, spending most of the time gazing out his window. Moose thumped him at one point, trying to get him to lighten up. But Jelly is Jelly, and when he goes silent, only *he* knows when he'll be back. Not that Moose and I were chatting it up. Except for the time it took to flip the cassette tape in the stereo, we'd been rockin' our way south; first to The Boss and then Lynyrd Skynyrd.

A deafening guitar duel bewailed the final crescendo of the fourteen-minute, thirty-eight-second "Live" version of *Free Bird.* The crowd's roar faded as we came over a little rise in the highway and the scattered lights of Santo Tomas came into view.

"I'm hungry. Let's get some tacos." Moose is never, not hungry.

"Tacos? Before breakfast?" I asked.

"You're in Mexico now, Opters. Tacos *are* breakfast." Jelly speaks! Maybe his unexplained sulking is over with.

"It's four thirty in the morning. Nothing's gonna be open."
I can drive for hours without eating or peeing, and this feels
way too soon to stop.

"C'mon, there's a bitchin' little restaurant right on the
main road that's always open. Real, Santo Tomas–style food.
I'll show you where to park." Moose's emphasis on the last
sentence made further objection fruitless.

"What's so special about Santo Tomas' Mexican food?"

"The difference is, we're *in* Santo Tomas now, and me and
Jelly are hungry. Hey! There it is! Pull in over there!"

"Whatever."

Moose was right about the place being open. It sat just
off the side of the road, lit up like an all-night bingo hall, two
clusters of floodlights and an orangish-red "Abierta, 24 Horas"
sign flashing sporadically in the window. Despite the neon
fanfare, it was a tiny place, the front part of a modest home
converted into a dining room for travelers.

Peering out through a gap in the window signage, a gray-
haired man who looked to be in his seventies, spotted us
pulling in and made his way to the door. He swung the door
wide and greeted us before we could climb out of the Bus.

"¡Buenos días, amigos! Come in, come in. We have the
best breakfast for you!"

He seemed so genuinely excited to see us, I cynically
wondered how long it'd been since the last person actually
pulled over and stopped here. Oh well, at least he knew a little
English; maybe he wouldn't screw up my order.

"¡Buenos días, my bueno amigo!" Even *I* recognized
Moose's Spanish was brutal, albeit better than the rest of ours.

"This way. This way. I have a very nice table for you."

I wondered to myself, which of the three was his, "very
nice table?"

Moose led, then Jelly; I brought up the rear. But then, I wouldn't have stopped here in the first place. At the moment I stepped across the threshold, everything went dark in the place. Unable to see a thing in front of me, I stopped in my tracks and looked over my shoulder. The whole town was dark. Every direction. No lights. Pitch-fucking-black.

The sound of a drawer opened too far—its contents crashing to the floor—snapped my head back around to the ink-black in front of me.

"¡Pinche luz!" an old woman's voice muttered in the darkness.

A match-strike flared, illuminating the room for a few seconds before fading. A flashlight clicked on. The old guy who'd met us at the front door held the light under his chin, his face now that of a friendly boogeyman. The shadow of an enormous head bearing an exaggerated nose filled the spotlight on the ceiling above him.

"No problema, my friends. We have our *own* lights to cook your meal."

I hadn't moved, still straddling the threshold. The old man aimed his light at my feet and did a "come hither," beckoning me to the table.

"You sit, Señor. You sit here now, and we make you the best breakfast." You had to give the guy credit. He was staying focused on the customer.

The lady with the matches lit a candle made from a baby abalone shell filled with wax and set it on our table. The old guy produced another, lit it from the first, and the room was beginning to feel almost normal again. Two young girls, probably all of six and eight years old, came through the kitchen door, each holding a tiny penlight. An older girl, maybe thirteen or so, shadowed the first two and carefully positioned the younger kids near our table. One behind Moose's chair, and one behind Jelly's. She took hold of each of the younger kids in turn and aimed their lights, before taking up position behind my chair with her own penlight. Now, each of us had our own personal assistant in place to help us see our menus.

Wow. Do they have these kids on standby? ... Or are they always dressed and awake at four-freakin'-thirty in the morning? It *was* cute though; the effort the whole clan's making to close this sale.

Three cups of hot, black coffee arrived at the table, delivered by yet another young girl. Probably fifteen or sixteen and very pretty, her silky, jet-black hair in two, waist-length braids completed with tiny bows of yellow string. She seemed terribly shy and averted her eyes each time I looked at her. The old man returned with a small juice glass, half-filled with tannish-colored liquid, and an old ceramic teacup brimming with a mound of coarse, off-white granules. He presented them with just a hint of flair, placing them both center stage on our table.

"Café con crema y azúcar... Coffee with cream and sugar, my friends." His eyes offered a disarming twinkle, enhanced by the candlelight. He seemed genuinely unfazed by the lack of electricity as he retreated to his kitchen.

This, the first moment with only our young light bearers at the table, I leaned in and whispered to the others, "Holy crap, you guys! Have you ever seen a family so desperate to make a buck before?"

Moose glanced at each of the kids in succession, checking to see if they understood what I had just said, before letting me have it.

"You're fucked up, Opters. You have no concept of what this culture is. These are simple people. This is all about helping us and being good hosts. That's how the people are brought up down here. They don't want to lose face by not being able to serve us, just because the power went out. That's why they busted out the candles and flashlights. They'll probably spend more on batteries and candles than they'll charge us for the food. What's important to them is that they show the kids the right way to treat a guest in their home."

The old man reappeared holding a pen and a napkin on which to take our orders. Stunned by Moose's reaction and subsequent reaming, I unconsciously tuned out the table talk and didn't hear a thing until it was my turn to order.

"Señor? Señor? What is your order, amigo?"

"Uhh … I'll have what they're having." *I feel the heat of every eye in the room on my face, even the kids.*

"We each got something different, Opters." said Jelly, bailing me out.

Pointing to Jelly this time, I tried to recover gracefully. "I'll have everything the same as him."

My turn to go quiet with my thoughts, as the guys joked and laughed their way through breakfast. Moose gave an impromptu tutorial on what he claimed to be the "official" Mexican method of using small pieces torn from a corn tortilla as your lone utensil. Our meal complete, the check arrived. Moose did the math, put his share with the check, and passed it to Jelly.

"Two fifty each, you guys. Plus, I think we should each put in an extra dollar for all the trouble these guys had to go to for us. What do *you* think, Opters?"

Jelly snickered and did another of his stupid Three Stooges imitations. "Yeah, Opters. Whadaya think, huh? Ack-ack-ack-ack." Jelly recently had become obsessed with the Three Stooges; he watched them every day and mimicked their routines and dialog ad nauseam. I think he actually felt a sort of perverse comfort in watching us all cringe each time he broke into the shtick. Perhaps it was his way of keeping his guard up; he was handsome and had a beautiful girlfriend, but seemed to freeze up awkwardly in social situations. Perro and I had watched it play out at parties, and we concluded his confident persona was only skin deep. His was a false bravado; when put on the spot, his insecurities betrayed him.

Jelly added his money to the Moose's, and laid the mix of bills and coinage in front of me. Not having any singles, I picked up the stack to make change for my ten-dollar bill. *Two fifty plus two fifty plus an extra dollar from each ... should be seven dollars here ... but, there's only six dollars.*

Fucking Moose. Yeah, let's each put in an extra dollar for the special service ... *I'll look like a dick if I bring it up now.* I pocketed the five singles and four quarters and laid the ten-dollar bill on the table. *Whatever.*

"Muchas gracias, Señores! Thank you for coming, my friends!" The old guy hadn't missed a beat.

The kids re-aimed their penlights and lit our path to the door. The old woman stepped from the kitchen to watch us leave. We exited single file, reprising our entrance of a half an hour ago; Moose, then Jelly, then me. With supernatural timing, the town's electricity came back on at the precise instant my rear foot left the building.

The old man brought his hands together in a clap, and with a toothy grin exclaimed, "You see my friends? A good breakfast will change your luck."

The youngest of the girls wriggled out between the old man and the door and called to us, "Vayan con Dios! Adiós Señores. Vayan con Dios!"

"Oh yes, my friends. Vayan con Dios." The old man's eyes rolled skyward, and he cradled his chin for a moment, contemplating the translation. A wide, kind smile washed over his face. "May your travels be with God at your side. Sí, Señores ... Vayan con Dios."

CHAPTER 5

THE BEST LAID PLANS

Hold the paraquat

There had been a palpable undercurrent of urgency during our trip planning sessions. Certainly, I had my *own* reasons to "get on with it"—never being 100 percent sure that a knock on my door by the Coronado Police Department wasn't forthcoming.

After Perro spilled the beans about Moose's flight from justice, I understood why the guy was so damn insistent about our "drop-dead" day for leaving. Plus, he'd surfed La Ticla once before and had been unrelenting with us about how perfect the waves were there in late summer. Left to Moose, we may as well have gone somewhere else if we hadn't headed south by the first of September.

Disguised in Three Stooges' shtick, Jelly had backed Moose's every call: When to leave, why the hurry, which route to take, where to camp along the way, how long to stay. "Yeah, … that's the ticket Moose! Ack-ack-ack-ack …" Jelly's motivations weren't apparent, but he was Moose's "second" on every vote. With two months allotted for this adventure, I pointed to all sorts of places that looked interesting on the map, only to be overruled at every turn. There are dozens of killer surf destinations all the way down the coast of Baja California, but we were on a mission to the mainland. There'd be no stopping. Even pulling off the road to *look* was verboten until we had reached La Ticla: the "Tropical Paradise" that Moose's tales had elevated to a near mystical place in our imaginations.

Choosing Baja was predicated on more than selecting a convenient entry point to the south. Traveling the length of the peninsula allowed us to bypass a three-hundred-mile section of mainland highway that traversed the heart of an agricultural area well-known for growing marijuana. President Jimmy Carter's DEA was actively crop-dusting vast tracts of the herb with their latest "War-on-Drugs" weapon, paraquat. Promoted as rendering marijuana toxic to the user—and therefore unappealing to a generation of potheads—paraquat spraying had become a highly publicized (and somewhat controversial) program.

None of us was a stranger to burning herb. Most of it was kick-your-ass pot, with names like "Acapulco Gold," "Panama Red," "Maui-wowie," "Inca Brown," or "Oaxacan" ("wo-hawk-in"). We coined our own name for paraquat-treated plants. We dubbed it "Commercial-wa-khan." It was the true "dirt-weed" of dope—and the *last* thing we wanted—was to be suspected of smuggling it. With the late-summer harvest approaching, we figured three twenty-something surfers, in an old VW Bus (with paisley-print curtains and California plates), would be too easy a target for the Federales to pick on.

To bypass the enforcement zone, we would stick to the Baja California Peninsula. Our route would take us due south all the way to the sleepy little fishing town of Cabo San Lucas, ensconced on the southernmost tip of land at the point where the warm Gulf of California waters collided with colder Pacific Ocean currents. Once there, we would board an ocean-going ferryboat for the fourteen-hour, open-water crossing, southeast to Puerto Vallarta on the mainland's Pacific coast. Ferryboats to the mainland departed a little farther up the coast at La Paz, too, but we'd decided the more time we spent on dry land, the better. Besides—with an abundance of fanfare—Mexico had proudly trumpeted the completion of their new Transpeninsular Highway. It was touted in my AAA travel guide as "a safe and modern expressway, linking the border metropolis of Tijuana to the city of La Paz, and onward to the quaint fishing villages of the South Cape ..." As we'd soon discover, the Transpeninsular Highway was a hodge-podge collection of freshly re-oiled two lane roadway, bridging countless bits of small town streets, roller-coaster runs of desert highway, and rutted mountain roads; an eleven-hundred-mile mosaic of dirt, gravel, asphalt, and concrete, zigzagging from north to south.

Disembarking the ferryboat in Puerto Vallarta, we would head south along the yet-to-be-completed "Mexican Coastal Expressway." According to Moose, construction of the new highway had stopped abruptly at the Ostula River, immediately north of our ultimate destination: La Ticla. Duly anointed the "Lime Capital of the World" by AAA, Tecomán would serve as our last stop for purified drinking water, hot showers, telephones, gasoline, groceries, and medical aid. Once we departed there, on the last two-hour leg to La Ticla, we *truly* were going to be on our own.

Karma's tipping points – Strike 3: Jelly comes clean

We were half an hour down the road from our breakfast stop and it was beginning to get light out. The pre-dawn sky was beautiful. Random thoughts skipped through my mind:

Hmm, it's Friday morning, September 1st, 1978. Moose will be a wanted fugitive in a few hours. How does he cross back into the U.S. without getting busted? I wonder if he's even thought it through that far. I hope Perro keeps an eye out for Dan-O lurking around The Manor. That guy gives me the willies. What's the big secret Jelly's keeping from us? What "promise" was Sherri screaming at him about?

The music had been off for a few minutes and, in the relative quiet, an observation struck me: I didn't know if we were tired, numb, bored, relieved, or concerned, but at the moment, we embodied the camaraderie of three strangers in an elevator.

"Fucking Sherri."

Well now … that gets Moose and my full attention!

"I mean, who told her to go off the pill, anyway?" Jelly had the floor. "All that bullshit last night? She was throwin' a fit about not being pregnant anymore."

Okay, … color me confused. Against my better judgement … "Whadaya mean, Jelly?"

"I mean she *was* pregnant and now she's *not*, Opters."

"Oh."

"She's been pregnant since June. You've seen her hanging 'round all the time, like we're married or something, haven't you?"

"Well, … yeah, but I …"

"I don't know why she didn't just get an abortion when it first happened. … I mean, who the fuck told her I wanted to start a family? You'd think after six years of being together, she'd have it figured out."

Six years? No shit she should have him figured out. Like, the guy's an ass to you and he's never going to be anything but an ass to you.

"So, she tells me two weeks ago that she wants to move in together and have the baby. She's gotta be outta her fucking mind."

My sentiments, exactly. The moving in together part, anyway.

"So, I tell her she better get the abortion before it's too late. I gave her the money for it and everything. I mean, I guess it was my responsibility to do that much anyway. And what do I get for doing the right thing? She freaks out on me."

Wow. He thinks that's the way to step up and take responsibility. What a guy.

"I made the mistake last week, of letting her know about this trip."

We've been planning this trip to Mexico for a month, and Sherri just found out last week? Think the "mistake" could've been not telling her sooner? Who are these people?

"When she freaked about me goin' to Mex, I gave her an ultimatum. You know, … a yes or no, what's it gonna be? kinda choice. I told her that if she had the abortion, I wouldn't go on this trip, and we'd use the money to look for a place."

"How come you never told *me* you were thinking of bailing out, Jelly?"

Moose … sounding hurt?

"I only did it to push her to get the abortion. I was never gonna bail on you. You're my bro, Moose. Bros before bitches, man. … You know how it is."

"So she did it? She had an abortion?" *How do I not sound incredulous?*

"No shit, Opters. You're a fucking master of the obvious. What do you think all the hysterics were about last night?" Moose answered for Jelly.

Wow, … I wonder where all this falls on the grand scale of moral equivalency? Ripping off your employer and trashing a family's precious home movies? Ducking out on jail time for manslaughter? Conning your girlfriend into aborting your baby?

A shot across our bow

BLAM! What the fuck was that? A backfire?

An idiot warning light glowed brightly near the bottom of my speedometer.

BLAM! There it was again. Yep, that's a backfire, alright. Let's see. … Red light is for "fan belt,"… white means "oil."

BLAM! "Goddammit *Opters*! What the hell is wrong with it?" Jelly seemed as panicked as I was.

"I don't know, but I gotta shut it off before it blows up or something."

Clutch in, key off, take it out of gear. … One last *BLAM!* lets rip, louder than the rest … and then, only the sound of our tires. The engine was still now, and we were coasting down a long, easy grade. I didn't know what to say; Moose and Jelly were looking at me, plainly expecting some kind of answer.

"The oil light is on … I have no clue whaa … the GODDAMN OIL LIGHT IS ON!"

I hope this isn't as bad as it feels like it's gonna be.

We strayed left across the centerline of the two-lane road and off the side into what passed as a pullout. Moose and Jelly stayed put like senior citizens on a tour bus, while I hopped out and walked to the rear to check under the hood. I didn't have to open the hatch to know we were in trouble. Dark puddlets traced our route from the highway and everything glistened with an iridescent sheen. Oily rainbows betrayed a slow migration of the precious lubricant toward the bumper, where it rallied and fell as a liquid metronome to the tailpipe below, each drop briefly sizzling until smoked out of existence. Moose emerged from the barn doors with a grunt and came around to see first-hand what was up.

"Is it bad?"

Jeeze, Moose, what was your first clue?

I knew it could be a blown engine, but I sugarcoated it for the moment, "I don't know what it is. We must have lost a seal or something, 'cuz there's oil coming from everywhere."

Moose's family owned a tire and brake shop since he was old enough to walk. He'd probably worked as many hours at *his* old man's business as I had at *mine*. He never really spoke of it much, but you got the idea he hated his father for it. I'd asked him one time about what life was like in jail. He said it beat the shit out of working at his dad's tire shop.

I'd been there once. Moose needed to get something at the tire shop and I'd given him a ride. The five minutes we spent in his dad's presence, I don't recall Mr. Moss speaking ten words to us, and the first half dozen were a growled, "What the fuck do you want?" To say he'd been forcibly overdosed on working on cars as a kid, would be understating the issue. Still, at this moment, Moose seemed to know instinctively what needed to be done and took charge of the situation.

"If it's lost all its oil, we gotta get some back in it while it's still hot or it's gonna seize. I know you brought a couple extra quarts of oil, Opters. Bring 'em to me, now."

A couple extra quarts? Hell, I had a case of twelve stashed under the bed. I ducked into the side door, fished out three quarts, and ran them back to Moose. He already had the hatch open and was fumbling with the dipstick.

"OUCH! Goddammit! This thing's hotter than crap!"

Not thinking, I pulled my T-shirt off over my head and handed it to him.

"Git on, Opters. Now you're gettin' with the program!" He took my shirt and used it to withdraw and check the dipstick. "No oil."

No shit, Sherlock. I could've saved you the trouble of checking, 'CUZ IT'S ALL OVER THE FREAKIN' GROUND!!!

He twisted off the filler cap and poured in a quart, tossed the empty aside, and dumped in another before checking the dipstick again. Again, none showed on the stick.

"Fuck, Opters, how long has the fucking light been on?"

"It just came on … I think … I don't know for sure … I was listening to Jelly … How the hell should I know how long it was on before I saw it?"

"Well, it's a good thing you have these three extra quarts, 'cuz if this is gonna work, it's gonna take every bit of it."

"I brought twelve."

"Git on."

The third quart finished draining into the filler, and Moose replaced the cap with a quarter-turn twist. "Go start it up."

"You sure, Moose?" I was a little skeptical that simply pouring in some fresh oil would get us going again.

"You got another plan?"

He has a point.

I climbed back behind the wheel, closed my eyes, and mouthed a silent, "Come on, God. Please?" before turning the key. It fired right up like nothing ever happened and ran smooth as silk.

"YEAH!!!! YEAH!!!!" Jelly and I yelled, giving each other high fives, and laughing.

"Hey, not so fast. Check it out." Moose said, pointing to underneath the engine. Trickling onto the dirt in a wispy, but steady flow, was fresh, amber-colored motor oil. "Okay, here's what we do." Moose let us know he was still in charge. "Engine's got a bad seal somewhere. We drive 'til the oil light comes on and pour another quart in. Once we see how far we can get before it needs another quart, we can figure out what the plan should be."

"You want to keep going *south?* It's eight hundred miles to La Paz. Wouldn't it be safer to backtrack to Ensenada?" *Seems logical to me …*

"C'mon Opters, let's at least see how far we get before it needs another quart. Don't you have extra parts and shit for this thing? We can stop at sundown, pull the engine, and fix it. You said yourself you can have it out in fifteen minutes."

I suppose Moose is right. I have every part we could need, and *I can drop the engine with my eyes closed* ... Fuck! ... *the jack. I let him talk me out of bringing the goddamned jack!*

"We don't have the jack. Remember?"

"You're wasting time and oil, Opters! Put this pig in gear and head south! We'll figure it out after we know how far a quart'll take us! GO!"

"Let's go, Opters. Don't worry. Moose knows what he's doing."

No surprise here. Jelly doesn't want to backtrack.

Pulling out, back onto the southbound side of the road, I accelerated gingerly, listening carefully for any hint of engine trouble. It sounded perfect.

"Odometer says 72,280 miles. Help me remember that, okay you guys?"

I spent more time staring at the idiot light on the dash the next few miles than I did the road. 72,288. Eight miles already. Maybe Moose was right about this after all.

"How 'bout some tunes, Opters?"

"I gotta listen to the engine, Jelly. No music 'til I know what's up."

The odometer rolled over 72,300.

"Wow. We've made it twenty miles already, you guys. Maybe this is gonna work."

72,310. In my own world, and visualizing the oil level dropping ever lower, I abruptly swerved left, right, left, right, and then left again, wanting to see if the warning light would glow if I swished the oil side to side. Caught completely off guard, Jelly lurched toward me briefly before overcorrecting, succumbed to the opposite inertia, and banged his head hard against the window. Before he could regroup, the right-left part of the cycle repeated, and his head thumped the window a second time.

I probably should've said something first.

"OW!!! Goddammit Opters! Whadaya doin'?!"

"Sorry, Jelly. I'm checking to see how the oil's doin'."

"Do that again and we're gonna be checking *your* oil!"

No light yet. I couldn't believe it, but everything seemed good. Another five miles ticked off and still no warning light.

"Okay guys, I'm gonna check the oil again."

Left-right-left-right-left. The oil light flickered as each left swerve oscillated into a right.

"We're there, you guys. Thirty-five miles on a quart. What do you think, Moose?"

Not waiting for an answer, I switched off the ignition and began coasting, looking for a good place to pull off the two-lane road. The engine quieted, the sounds of gravel crunching beneath the tires grated against the silence as we rolled off the shoulder and slowed to a stop. Moose muttered something under his breath and spread the map across his lap. I figured he had some math to do, so I grabbed a fresh quart and headed to the back to give the engine another drink.

"Gloop, gloop, gloop, gloop …" The sound of the thick liquid glugging from the bottle seemed out of place in the still vastness of the Baja desert. A grunt from around front announced Moose's exit from the 1DRBUS, an ill-folded map choked in a fist at his side.

"How's it look?"

"Seems like it's running okay. Just a bunch of oil everywhere."

"Let's gas up in Guerrero Negro. After that, the first town we come to with any real shade is Santa Rosalía—like, 270 miles from here. We'll stay there overnight, pull the engine and fix it. We can be back on the road by morning, and still make the ferry that leaves Cabo Sunday."

"There's no shade between *here* and Santa Rosalía? We're running on a wing and a prayer as it is, Moose. Why do we have to push it all the way to eff-ing Santa Rosalía?"

"No ... there's not." Moose was adamant. "The road turns east at Guerrero Negro. Nut'n but little towns and desert 'til we cross over to the gulf. Don't worry about it. There'll be places we can get more oil if we need it. C'mon, let's go another thirty-five miles."

Another thirty-five miles? Nothing but desert? Where's the "more oil" going to come from, Jed Fucking Clampett? Mustn't show panic. We still have eight quarts on board. Even if we don't find more oil, we'll make it the 270 miles to Santa Rosalía. Right GOD?

"Okay, Moose."

The next 140 miles went by in one-quart chunks, paced by "left-right-left-right-left" swerves every few miles, and dusty little towns every thirty or forty. Instead of sixty-five miles an hour with the stereo blasting, we poked along in silence at fifty. The miles dragged by. The desert seemed to go on forever in every direction. We hadn't had a glimpse of water since the big turn at Guerrero Negro. And *that* felt like it was three days ago.

"Less than a hundred miles to Santa Rosalía, Moose. I think we're gonna make it, but it'll be dark before we get there." The sun already was low in the sky behind us, as we headed almost due east across the peninsula. "Think we should stop somewhere before there and get on with pulling the engine?"

"Nah ... Even if we stopped right now, it'll be dark before the thing's cool enough to work on." Moose wasn't about to deviate from his plan without an argument. "Let's just get there."

Feeling every bit the subordinate, I grumbled under my breath, "It's gonna be hard *enough* fixing the engine in daylight ...," but decided to let it go for now. Scarcely two minutes later, the oil light flickered its warning.

"Something's up, you guys. The eff-ing oil light is on and it's only been fifteen miles since the last quart. Hang on." A quick left-right-left confirmed it. We needed another quart already.

"That sucks. I think the leak is getting worse. We gotta stop and pull it, Moose, or we won't have enough oil to put back in when we're done."

With the warning light glowing brightly now, I couldn't afford to wait for anyone's blessing and flicked off the ignition. Short another option, I steered the 1DRBUS over the jagged shoulder and onto the desert hardscrabble. There was no more than a random weed growing nearby, and though it was already well past 7 p.m., the brutal afternoon heat persisted. Lacking a wisp of wind, the dust raised by our stopping hung overhead, suspended by the heat rising off the desert floor. A drop of oil heralded its arrival on the muffler with an audible sizzle. A faint haze of bluish smoke tinted the scene in my side-view mirror. Gazing at the heat-distorted horizon, I pondered which was hotter, the engine or the gravel?

The pack's been pinched

Apparently, none of us wanted to be the first to exit. We sat, fairly cooking inside the Bus, sensing the reality: It was even *more* oppressive outside. Our apprehension and dismay overwhelmed the heavy air. I allowed several more moments to pass, then trudged to the rear to take inventory of our situation. Okay, let's see here. ... No shade. No jack. Haven't seen another vehicle in an hour. The engine is smokin' hot and my flip-flops are sticking to the ground beneath my feet. *Fuck this.* Back to the front, I reunited my board shorts with the steaming green vinyl of the driver's seat.

"Check the map, Jelly. How far to the next town where we can get more oil?"

"Whatsamatta, change your mind?"

"Nahhh. It's just too fucking hot out there to even think about working on the engine for a while. We might as well keep going. Especially if it means stopping somewhere better than here for the night." *Anywhere's gotta be better than here, right?*

"Let's do it now." Moose cut in. "C'mon. We gotta do it now. Too much oil has leaked out jus' sittin' here. It'd be a waste to fill it again without fixin' it. We're committed."

"Whaaa ...?" *Now it's my fault for stopping? Whatever. I'd rather know it's fixed, than keep stressing about burning it up, anyway.*

"Okay Moose. But it'll be at least an hour or two before the engine is cool enough to work on."

"Bullshit. We're gonna do it now. We got rags and water, right?"

"Well ... ya, rags ... but ..."

"C'mon. I'm gonna show you. My dad taught me how to work on a hot engine."

Now, there's a skill I'd hoped I'd never need. Fine, Moose. You show me. You do the whole fucking thing, 'cause I'm not getting near an engine cranking out smoke signals!

"Grab your tools, and let's get this goin'." With that, Moose pulled his T-shirt over his head, reverently draped it across the back of his seat, and headed back to the engine compartment, bare chested and looking primed for a fight.

"Opters, grab a jug of water and soak a couple o' rags real good."

Hmm ... First step must be, "Wipe some of the oil off."

I did as I was told and soon reappeared at the rear, toolbox in one hand, a clutch of dripping rags in the other. "Here you go, Moose."

"No gloves?"

"Didn't bring any."

"Then grab four socks, and soak 'em good."

"What're they for Moose?" *I'm getting a bad feeling about this.*

"They're for our hands. I told you, I'm gonna show you how we work on a hot motor."

Like pulling a string, my dad's oft-repeated correction played in my head and I parroted it without thinking, "It's an *engine*, Moose. *Motors* run on electricity; *engines* use gas." *This is not doing my quest for cooldom any good.* "More than that, it's an air-cooled engine; one that's lost all of its oil! Do you have any concept of just how fucking hot that thing is right now?"

"Quit yer snivlin', Mister Wizard, and get the goddamned socks!"

I looked to Jelly for help, but he just shrugged and averted his gaze, recognizing the folly of getting involved.

"Fuck it! I'll get 'em myself!" Moose bluffed toward the side door.

Foot-dragging is clearly no longer an option.

"I got it. I got it. I don't want you diggin' in my shit."

A couple of minutes later, "Scrub-Nurse Jelly" was pulling tube socks onto Moose and me like we're a pair of Sesame Street surgeons.

"Opters! Get your socks wet, and let's start stripping this pig down. No jack. ... Okay, ... Jelly! Go around front, pull the spare tire off and bring it back here."

Tentatively at first, Moose and I began by removing a series of small bolts holding a variety of tin pieces that shrouded the engine. Virtually everything we touched, bumped, or brushed against, sizzled or steamed. The hot desert air dried our makeshift oven mitts, the resulting coolness a welcome distraction from the miserable task at hand. Despite our tube-sock-induced lack of dexterity, we had the engine stripped and ready to drop in ten minutes.

Moose resumed barking out orders like a squadron-leader preparing us for a frontal assault. "C'mere, Jelly. Push that tire up under the engine, and get yourself some wet rags. Opters, you 'n' Jelly're gonna grab the exhaust and pull hard while you're jiggling it around. I'm gonna push the Bus forward. The engine is gonna drop on the tire. When it does, you guys need to keep it from tipping over and fucking somebody up."

"How 'bout I push the Bus, Moose? You 'n' Opters know more about how to grab the motor and everything."

"It's an engine Jelly." Moose flashed me a goofy grin. "Just ask Mr. Wizard here. Now, both you get your rags good and wet. That exhaust's still red hot and I don't want either of you pussin' out, lettin' go, and gettin' me burned."

Our first attempt was a bust. Crouching, Jelly and I grabbed the exhaust and began pulling with all our might. Without warning, Moose threw his shoulder into the Bus, ripped the exhaust from Jelly's hands, and yanked me onto all fours, the sharp gravel gouging the flesh of both knees.

"Ow, Moose! How 'bout a freakin' warning, or something?"

"Well, pay attention, goddammit!"

Now, there's a phrase I bet Moose learned from his dad early on.

Jelly chuckled and chin-bobbed in the direction of my fresh scrapes. "Nice ones, Opters."

"Way to hold on, Jelly."

At least the socks kept the palms of my hands from getting skinned as well. Regrouping for a second go, Moose had us both sit in the dirt and dig in our heels. With only the thin

71

fabric of boardshorts to shield our asses, the hot ground quickly became intolerable, and steam rose instantly from wherever our sock-protected hands touched the exhaust.

"On three, okay?"

"Fuck *that*, Moose! We're burning down here!"

"Thought you snivelers wanted a warning?"

"Fucking, PUSH already!!!"

"THREE!"

It was a miracle none of us were hurt. The engine broke free of its mounts and "kah-whumped!" onto the tire like a ninety-pound bag of concrete sliding off a roof.

Once it was out and the fan housing off, it was obvious where all the oil was coming from. In old Volksy engines, there's a little, black, metal skyscraper-shaped thing mounted on top of the block that helps cool the oil. Two little rubber donuts at the base of the skyscraper keep the oil from leaking out. One of mine was torn in half, sticking out like two pieces of a fat, green rubber band.

"Awesome, Moose!"

"What is?"

"Look there ... that seal is torn, and I have a brand-new set of 'em in with the spare parts."

"Git on, Opters! Get 'em, and let's get this pig back on the road!"

Feeling smugly full of myself, I dug past the spare fuel pump, extra distributor cap, virgin coil. Pushed aside a four-pack bundle of new spark plugs. Ahhh, ... there it was, in all its glory. One, cellophane-wrapped, cardboard-backed, pristine package; its Volkswagen baby-blue-and-white block lettering, practically screaming, "Engine seals. Master set for 1500cc VW engine." I grabbed it and marched triumphantly back to the rear of the Bus. Trying to keep it a notch below giddy, I Frisbee'd the pack to Moose. "Check it out."

"Git on, Opters. Let's see whatcha got." Moose pressed both thumbs to the cheap cellophane and split the seam running up the back, spilling the assortment of rubber, cork, and cardboard to the ground. Hardly the reverence I thought the seals deserved, but perhaps I lowered the bar by flipping the pack to him the way I had.

"I don't see 'em," Moose said, pawing through the pile with his chubby fingers.

"Yeah. That's the ticket … Ack-ack-ack-ack … No seals in the pack … ack-ack-ack-ack … No seals in the pack."

Not even a little bit funny, Jelly.

"No. *Really*, you guys, I don't fucking see 'em."

"Lemme look."

Yeah, like you know what to look for, Jelly.

"They *gotta* be there! Maybe you buried 'em the way you dumped everything in the dirt like that!"

"Fuck you, Opters. Look, I'm telling you, the pack's been pinched. The little donuts ain't here. We're fucked."

For the next ten minutes, first me, then Jelly, clawed, scratched, and kicked at the loose soil where the new seals and gaskets were scattered. Moose sat in the Bus, his feet poking out of the barn doors, mumbling and shaking his head. Sunset was upon us. A little while ago, it would've been cause for rejoicing, but now had become a major concern. We had the engine in pieces; lacked the parts to put it back together; it was getting dark soon. … AND WE WERE IN THE MIDDLE OF THE FUCKING DESERT!!!

"We gotta put it back in," Moose said.

"And then what?"

"And then we make it to the next town, Opters. I ain't about to spend the night out here waiting to get robbed."

"ROBBED? What the fuck are you talking about?"

"The banditos will know we're stuck. They'll know we have money 'cause we're pointed south. And, they'll know we can't do shit to stop 'em. If we don't get to some kind of town soon, we'll be sittin' ducks."

"Since when are there banditos out here in the middle of the desert?" I'm still waiting for the punch line.

"I'm serious, you guys. Just because they built this new road, doesn't mean they don't still rob gringos who are stupid enough to camp in the middle of nowhere."

"Opters. Can't you make something outta one of the other gaskets, or part of your swim fins, or something, that'll seal this pig up long enough to get us to Santa Rosalía?"

Well, not getting robbed and killed is certainly motivation to think of something, now isn't it?

"I ... I can try to make something out of one of the valve-cover gask ... No, that won't work ... maybe if I ... well ... I'll ... I'll try to make something that'll work, okay?"

I spent the next ten minutes rummaging through my things up front. I was on mental autopilot, contemplating what might contain the right material from which to create two new, pinky-ring-size "rubber doughnuts" as workable substitutes for the oil cooler seals. I was skeptical this was gonna work, but what did I have to lose ... well, except that I'd be sacrificing something I didn't think I could live without on this trip. *Yeah, there* is *that.*

Swim fins, dive mask, snorkel ... no way. I'm not going to end up on a tropical beach without the gear necessary to check out the reefs. Surfboard leash? Nope. Not with the kinda surf Moose has been talking about for as long as I can remember. Maybe there's part of the 1DRBUS I can cannibalize. ... Wait, I've got it! The movie camera has a couple of rubber lens caps; one for the front lens and another for the eyepiece. It sucks that I have to do this, but what are my other choices? Besides,

74

I rationalized, it came with a killer case that'll keep it safe, and I can always buy new lens caps when we get back to the States. So that's it. I'll make them work. I hope.

"Okay Moose. I got it. I'm gonna make 'em from these." Palm out, showing off what I found.

"Git on, Opters. Get going, so we can get this pig back on the road before we get robbed out here."

I didn't have enough brain cells free to stew on Moose constantly referring to the 1DRBUS as a pig, the threat of being robbed, *and* how I was gonna fashion two new oil cooler seals out of the movie camera's lens caps. I saved the first two for later, and set about carving up the caps.

It took a few minutes to trace the torn gaskets' shapes onto the rubber caps before I was ready to begin cutting them out. I figured I had only one shot at this, and there were no points for speed, only results.

Moose was getting impatient as the sky transitioned from purple to black. "Come on, Opters! Just make 'em already!"

"Hey, do you want 'em right ... or right now?" *Damn. That sounded "in charge." Cool!*

After a few trial fittings, a nick here, and a scrape there, I was satisfied the two makeshift seals were as good as could be crafted with razor blade and scavenged rubber.

"Okay, you guys. Let's put her back together." I felt like I should pause for a moment to thank God for supplying the materials, tools, and skill to pull this off, but rationalized that there really wasn't time for that now. I told myself I'd get to it later, once (and if) we were on the road again. The engine went back together without a hitch. Barely fifteen minutes later we were ready to mount it back in the 1DRBUS. *Damn it! We still don't have a jack, do we?*

"Hey, Moose. How do we get the engine back up onto its mounts?" *Hey ... he's the one who said he could get it out and put it back; I only said I could put it back together after taking it apart.*

"You worry too much. I got us covered." With that, he spread out a beach towel and lay on it, flat on his back, his head centered behind the open engine hatch.

This should be good.

"Jelly, you and Opters each grab one side of the engine, bring it over here, and set it on my chest, facing the right way."

"Okay Moose, if you say so, but it'll still be too low to reach the mounts and we can't raise it up on something because that'll make it too high to get past the hatch door."

Wow, I didn't think Jelly was paying attention to anything but Jelly.

"Here's what's gonna happen. You guys put the engine on my chest, then roll the Bus back 'til the engine is past the hatch door. Oh, and put some rocks against the tires so the Bus don't move. Then, I'm gonna bench press the engine up to where it can slip onto the mounting bolts. When I get it lined up, Jelly, you're gonna sit on your ass and kick the engine back onto the bolts."

That left me as odd man out. "What will I be doing, Moose?"

"You're gonna climb under the Bus with me and thread the nuts onto the mounting bolts as soon as the engine slides into place."

"I don't know about this, Moose."

"You got a better plan, or should we wait for the banditos to give us a hand?"

He's got a point.

Moose ran through the instructions one more time (guess he didn't want to be left pinned to the Baja desert by an engine setting on his chest), and then we got busy. Jelly and I strained to lift the engine and carried it the few feet to where Moose lay on his back. There was no way in hell that either of us could lift this thing by ourselves, and I was having a difficult time picturing Moose bench pressing it into the air (and holding it there) while Jelly and I assumed our positions, maneuvered the thing into place, and then located the bolts up under the chassis onto which the nuts needed to go … in the dark. Nevertheless, we did as we were told, and as gently as possible laid the engine onto Moose's chest. With the muffler digging into his belly and the flywheel pressed against his chin, he squeaked out a, "Go now! Go. Go!"

We pushed the Bus back over him, his lower half resembling road kill protruding from behind. Jelly got into position, ready for the signal to kick the engine back onto the bolts. I wormed my way in alongside Moose, with a mounting nut in each hand. It took a minute for me to wriggle in far enough that I'd be able to reach the places where the nuts belonged. Uncomfortably wedged between Moose and the inside of the left rear tire, my nose bumped against the underside of the engine lying across his chest. Both of my arms were stretched out above my head … I was, in a word: *defenseless.*

"Okay. I'm good. Can you lift it?" *My mother would kill me if she knew about this.* I didn't know whether to hope Moose could do it, or pray that he couldn't. Everything about this was freakin' insane.

Moose's chest swelled, then froze in place; his right elbow punched sharply into my ribs below my left arm pit. His legs went rigid, the veins in his neck bulged freakishly, and he bellowed a primal "Aggghh …!" that ignited an adrenaline-fueled fight-or-flight instinct, bordering on panic, deep inside of me. The engine wobbled and wove for a bit before shakily pushing away from our faces and into the dark void above it. All too quickly, the top of it met the ceiling of the engine compartment with a resounding, *thump.*

"You're too high. You gotta bring it back down a little." I didn't know how long he could hold it—much less lower it a couple of inches—and then hold it steady in that position. *That is precisely what jacks are for.*

"Whaaa …? How much lower, how much! Tell me when! Goddammit!" Moose's arms began to tremble as he lowered the engine in jerky increments. It started to sway from side to side as he struggled for control, his bench press now barely half extended.

"THERE, MOOSE! KEEP IT THERE! JELLY! KICK! KICK! KICK!"

Dear GOD, I hope it hits a bolt hole!

I didn't foresee him being able to bring the engine back down gently, and my face was between it and the ground. Jelly kicked the engine back, but the ends of the bolts were missing the holes. A little high one time, a little low the next, too far left, farther off to the left ….

Damn it!

"You okay, Moose? We're just missing by a tiny bit. Can you hold it any stiller?"

"Aggghhhh! You guys have five seconds before I'm gonna drop. FUCKING DO IT!!! AGGGGGGHHHHH!!!!"

With that, the engine slid home. A few flicks of my fingers spun the first nut snug, locking the beast safely in place. Moose's arms collapsed onto his chest like overcooked pasta. An uncharacteristically nervous giggle escaped him.

"You guys got it?" Jelly kicked my foot for an answer.

The two of us just lay there, too drained to move a muscle, Moose now chuckling between gasps, me gently shaking my head.

"Hey. Push it off us, okay? I don't think we can get out on our own."

Jelly obliged, and the underside of the engine gave way to the most intense, star-filled sky I'd ever witnessed. Still on our backs and gazing skyward, I was the first to interrupt the moment.

"Hey Moose, what were you laughing about just then?"

"I was thinking about how jail had saved my life. I mean, if I hadn't spent so much time lifting weights in there, I would've dropped that fucking thing on us."

Wow.

It took about ten minutes to reattach the tin, connect the wires, and put the rest of the stuff back in place, before we poured the last of our oil in and were ready to give the engine a try. It fired right up and purred like a kitten. No sign of oil leaking. *How cool is that?* We pulled back onto the highway and drove the hundred miles to Santa Rosalía at pretty much normal speed, stopping only once to confirm the oil was still in the engine where it belonged. Once in town, we found a place to park overnight. The guys set up outside, Moose in his bedroll on the ground and Jelly on his cot. I moved things around inside the 1DRBUS and folded out my full-size bed. Not much was said between us, all three too mentally and physically exhausted to do anything but crash for the night.

A case of "looo-bree-cawnt-Ā"

Moose was up at dawn and felt it his obligation to wake Jelly and me to share with us how sore his arms and chest were this morning.

"I think I pulled something last night. I can hardly lift my arms"

"I guess you'll just have to starve, then."

Good one, Jelly.

"So, how close were you to dropping that thing on our faces, Moose?"

"I wasn't gonna let it hit *my* face. The wires just came off my jaw. Fuck that. Hey, you guys ready to get something to eat before we get going?"

"I'm not that hungry. You guys go ahead." Picturing that thing crushing my skull took my mind right off of food. "Besides, I want to check a few things on the 1DRBUS before we hit the road again. And you know ... just in case ... I want to buy some more oil to take with us."

"Just in case of what, Opters?"

What? Did Jelly think that was all a dream?

Moose crossed his arms, massaging both biceps. "Naw, that's a good idea. The Mexicans call it Lubricante."

I'm so glad he knows some Spanish. This trip would be a lot tougher without him.

"How do you pronounce it, Moose? Say it a little slower, okay?"

"Looo-bree-cawnt-Ā."

"Okay, got it. Lubricante."

With that, the guys crossed the road toward a cluster of shops in search of breakfast, and I grabbed a rag to check the dipstick. Hmmm, not bad. Only down a smidgeon. Guess the lens caps are holding.

Maybe I should be an inventor or something.

Still, it took us every drop of oil we had to get here last night. I think I should pick up at least six or eight quarts. You know ... just in case. I didn't see anything remotely resembling an automotive supply store across the road, so I locked up and took off in the opposite direction from Moose and Jelly's.

Each storefront I passed was something foreign to me.

Imagine that, "foreign." Duh.

In the window of the first shop was a neon-tube caricature of a jug on its side, spilling liquid. The sign on the door said "Agua Pura." I was used to seeing a few shelves of bottled water at the supermarket, but a whole store dedicated to nothing but water? Next was a "Veterinaria" followed by "Farmacia," "Dentista," and then "Licorería." It was all so random. Or, perhaps not. I mean, having your choice of drugs or liquor on the way into, or out of the dentist's office might be useful.

The next few buildings only were partially completed and decaying in place. Or possibly they were once complete and are now being cannibalized of their materials? Hard to say for sure. I was running out of options, so I entered the next store, figuring I could at least ask them to point me in the right direction in my quest for Lubricante. Inside the humble shop it was an eclectic blend of: overloaded garage full of junk, candy shop, and toy store. Random hand tools hung on wire hoops fashioned from old coat hangers and nailed to a beam, high above the doorway. Colorful, cellophane-wrapped packages of what appeared to be chewing gum (and candies I'd never heard of) were organized into neat rows of little paper cartons along a counter by the window. Two worn bicycle tires, one very large and one obviously from the rear of a tricycle, hung from a metal tent spike wedged into a crack in the wood plank wall. A toy wagon, bearing several plastic, child-size garden implements, and a sun-bleached, orange-yellow-and-green toy lawn mower sat parked in the corner.

An old woman got up stiffly from behind the counter and didn't say a word, sizing me up with her eyes.

"¿Dónde está el lubricante, por favor?" *So my Spanish isn't perfect. With Moose's help, I oughta be able to get the point across, eh?*

She looked at me like I'm from Mars, "¿Qué?"

"¿Dónde está el lubricante, por favor? You know, … oil for *mi carro*." I don't have a clue what "mi carro" translates to, but hope it's something close enough for her to guess at.

Her expression somewhere between annoyed and perplexed, she just stared at me.

I hope I haven't unwittingly insulted her! This isn't going very well.

"¿Dónde está lubricante?" *Maybe she's an Indian and doesn't speak Spanish very well?* I tried it more slowly, carefully enunciating each syllable, "Looooo-breeee-cawwwnt-Ā."

"No está."

Yeah, I kinda gathered that from looking around your store, lady.

"Si. I know lubricanté no está. Where is … I mean, dondé es lubricanté?"

"¿Qué es?"

"¡Si! ¿Qué es lubricanté?" *She's making this a chore because my grammar is bad?*

She shook her head and silently retook her seat behind the counter.

I'm gonna need Moose for this …

It was a bit of a walk back the way I came, and the guys were already there, leaning against the side of the 1DRBUS.

"Where's your oil, Opters? We need to get this pig on the road."

"I couldn't find any, Moose. No one seems to know what lubricanté is, or maybe I'm just saying it wrong. I need you to ask."

"Let's just get on the road to Loreto. We should gas up and buy oil at the PEMEX on the way out of town. Besides, it's called *aceite*. I was just fucking with you. Did you have a good time? Breakfast was killer."

"Yeah, Opters. Breakfast was killer. Ack-ack-ack-ack."

Was Jelly in on it from the beginning, or just enjoying me looking the fool? I don't care either way. They're both assholes.

CHAPTER 6

WE HAVE TWO OF THE BEST...

White crosses and purple dingle balls

So, like Moose said we could, we bought a case of oil from the PEMEX at the south end of town and were on our way. Except for being annoyed and a little hungry, the next three hours were paradise. I was beginning to relax and enjoy the journey, as the highway skirted along the most beautiful lagoons and seashore I'd ever seen. The colors of the rocks, sand, and water were almost too much to absorb. The occasional grouping of white-painted crosses and flowers on either side of the roadway served to remind me to keep my eyes on the road. I wondered for a moment how many years it had taken to accumulate so many makeshift monuments to the inattentive motorist. When there was a grouping of a dozen or more crosses in one location, was it memorializing one big horrific accident, or merely a particularly dangerous, and frequently missed, curve in the road?

We gassed up again in Loreto and continued south until the highway took a dramatic westward turn away from the gulf and began a steady, winding climb into the mountains.

83

You'd think that going higher, it would get cooler out, but moving away from the water had the opposite effect. Bearable all morning, the air became heavy, hot, and overpowering once more. The only thing moving the air was us driving through it. Moose was snoring in the back; Jelly slouched down in the passenger seat in a vain effort to find a comfortable place to rest his head. I leaned forward, my elbows on the steering wheel, trying my best to keep my back clear of the hot, dark-green vinyl upholstery, which stuck to my bare skin whenever given the chance. I downshifted into third gear as the grade grew steeper and the road narrowed, reducing our already painfully slow pace.

"Hey Jelly. Why do you think there are so many crosses along our side of the road, and none on the downhill side?"

Before he could answer, a bus came around the corner going way too fast and laying on his horn. In a strange, time-warped moment, I made eye contact with the driver—perfectly framed in a wiper-blade's swath of an otherwise mud-streaked windshield—a row of tiny (alternating purple and green) dingle balls dancing above his head. With a reflexive "holy shit!," I slid two tires as far onto the shoulder as I dared, the steep drop-off on our side wholly unprotected, save for a tidy row of white-washed rocks defining the edge. The bus careened by, the proximity of its draft pulling the 1DRBUS even farther into its path for a terrifying split second.

"What the fuck, Opters! You trying to get us killed? That bus nearly got us!"

"Yeah, I saw that, Jelly." I deadpanned.

Behind us, Moose stirred awake. "Why we stopping?"

"Opters almost ran us into a bus."

"What're you talking about? He took up the whole damn road and nearly ran us off the cliff! I gotta check the tires. We hit some of those effing rocks pretty hard."

With that, I turned off the engine, hopped out, and walked around the front to the passenger side to take a look. Front tire looks okay. Same with the rear. *Ahh shit. Oil.*

"We're leaking oil again. Lots of it."

"From a rock?" asks Jelly.

"I don't think so. Same place as before. I think it's those damn seals. Engine probably got too hot going up these effing mountains and melted the lens caps. It's kinda weird it happened precisely at this moment."

The last few minutes feels like a *Twilight Zone* episode.

"You guys think maybe that bus was timed to get us to pull over before we burned up the engine? Whatever … I'm glad we have a fresh case of oil to get us to the next PEMEX."

"We can't stay here, half on the road and everything. Put some oil in and let's get this pig over the hill."

Hey, there's an idea, Moose. Get over the pass, turn off the engine, and coast down the other side!

And so we did. Add oil. Drive a bit. Coast whenever possible. Repeat. All the way to the VW dealership in La Paz, about 175 miles away. Now, 175 miles doesn't sound that far, but it took another *twenty-six* quarts of oil, the rest of the day, and into the night to make it.

Down to our last quart, and too risky to go any farther, we set up camp in front of Volkswagen La Paz, Baja California Sur. Located at the intersection of the Transpeninsular Highway and the main boulevard in downtown La Paz, we were a sight to see. The guys hung their mosquito netting off the side of the 1DRBUS and stretched it over the heavy chain that restricted entry to the service garage driveway. Out came the ice chests, Moose's bedroll, and Jelly's cot. We fired up the stove and cooked a late dinner of canned ham and baked beans.

Locals honked and called out to us. Moose's Spanish was tested, trying his best to explain to police officers what it was we were thinking—camping *here*. Pointing out the thick coating of motor oil all over the back of the 1DRBUS did the best job of filling in the blanks. They let us stay—likely because they felt sorry for us—and guessed that we weren't about to get very far if forced to leave. But they also made it abundantly clear that this was a *one-night-only* kind of deal, and we'd better find a campground to stay at after this. As I drifted off to sleep, I was thinking about how I couldn't remember what color the bus was that nearly ran us off the cliff, but the tiny purple and green dingle balls framing the driver's face were as clear as day.

Between Moose and a meal

Just after first light, the *bang-bang-bang-bang!* of a hand sharply slapping the side of the 1DRBUS fractured the dawn air. A few seconds pause, and another *bang-bang-bang-bang!* Moose muttered something unintelligible in any language. The mosquito netting lifted in the middle to reveal a serious looking, middle-age man wearing a crisp blue shirt and black trousers, a "VW" insignia over one shirt pocket and an embroidered patch, "Roberto Nueves, Administrador de Auto Servicio" over the other. The three of us needed a moment to gather our senses and remember where we were—and what we were here for.

For the next few minutes, the service manager patiently endured Moose's tortured Spanish. When he saw the oil slick all over the rear of the Bus, Roberto tacitly understood that we had limped our way to him from a bit north of San Quintin, spewing oil for more than eight hundred miles. I thought it funny he didn't ask why we hadn't turned around and gone back to Tijuana. Or, better yet, home to San Diego.

Roberto was positively beaming that we had struggled so mightily to reach *his* VW service department, and now *he* was going to be the hero and save the day! Once he'd fully digested that we went through thirty-eight quarts of oil to reach his garage, he put his hand up: "Un momentito, por favor." The mechanics had begun showing up for the day's work in groups of two and three. Roberto called each arriving party over and, in an excited tone, relayed our story to them. Understanding the language wasn't necessary. When he reached the part about the thirty-eight quarts of oil and the last eight hundred miles of our trek, the big eyes, shaking heads, and laughter told it all. Moose dug out about ten of his dirty magazines, gave two of them to Roberto, and (getting his okay) distributed the rest to the mechanics gathered around us.

After the obligatory paperwork, our new best friend, Roberto, asked us where we'd be staying, because he expected it to take until closing the next day to complete the repairs, and he couldn't permit us to camp at the dealership another night.

Shit, we had the engine out, torn apart, put back together, and back in the Bus in less than ninety minutes ... in the dark, in the middle of the desert, without a jack! Now they want it for almost two full days! Oh well, at least it will be done, and with the right parts.

Since we had no idea of where to go, Roberto had us load our gear into the back of his pickup truck and carted us to the outskirts of town, to what he said was an "authorized campground." Really it was more of a dusty parking lot— ringed on three sides with barbed wire—than it was a campground. Six or seven dilapidated travel trailers, a few decrepit looking sheds, and two small corrugated-tin shelters that looked like they'd been erected to shade livestock. No electricity. No running water. A lone porta potty stood about fifty yards from the nearest trailer, through a gap in the barbwire fence.

Gee, I can hardly wait to take a dump in there *in the afternoon heat!*

A tiny, sun-wrinkled old man, wearing only faded black swim trunks and a beat up pair of rubber flip-flops, emerged bare chested from one of the trailers. After a brief conversation with Roberto, he pointed to one of the two tin-roofed shelters and held up three fingers. Roberto said something to Moose in Spanish, and Moose turned to us,

"He wants a dollar apiece for one night."

Everyone looked at me, so I dug three singles from my pocket and handed them over to our host. He folded the bills several times, tucked them into his waistband, and disappeared back into his small trailer, needing to slam the door twice to get it to latch.

With a broad smile and an exaggerated wave of his hand, Roberto motioned toward our tin shelter with a cheerful sounding *"Tu casa"* ("Your house") and said that he'd come for us as soon as the repairs to the 1DRBUS were completed.

It's only 9 in the morning and it has to be 100 degrees in the shade already. Marooned here in the middle of nowhere, we helplessly watched him drive away.

Jelly set up his cot while Moose and I did our best to clear the pebbles, weeds, and stickers from a patch of earth large enough to accommodate our bedrolls. The occasional, large red ant trekked across the hard-packed dirt, in search of something worthy of alerting the colony to. A squadron of flies patrolled overhead in well-defined angular patterns, taking refuge from the direct sun.

"Hey Opters, how's it feel not having your big old custom-made bed to sleep in? I bet my cot is looking pretty good to you about now, eh?"

"Yeah Jelly, whatever. I'll be back in my bed tomorrow and you'll still be lying on your stupid cot."

"How 'bout you, Moose? Don't you wish you had been smart enough to bring a cot? How are the ants down there?"

"Fuck you *and* your cot. I'm gonna put boogers on you as soon as you're asleep, and then we'll see who the ants like best." With that, Moose turned on his side and let rip a long, loud fart in Jelly's direction.

I think I'll steer clear of this skirmish.

The second shoe dropped about five seconds later when the first wave of Moose's aromatic assault reached Jelly. In a single movement, he put his hand to his face, thrust his legs out, and lurched upright on his prized Army Surplus Store cot. The sound that followed was of a quick pull on a long zipper, as the old canvas split under him, dropping him butt-first to the dirt below.

I don't think I'd ever laughed so hard in all my life. Moose was drooling and tearing up. Neither of us was able to complete a coherent sentence. A few minutes into it we were clutching our stomachs to sooth the cramping. Jelly didn't say another word the rest of the afternoon. He refused to acknowledge defeat, instead sliding first one, and then a second, ice chest lengthwise under each end of the ripped cot before remaking his bed atop them. I had been jealously guarding my film to memorialize our escapades in La Ticla, but unable to resist this Kodak moment, I snapped a picture of Jelly on his improvised bunk. Just too damn funny to pass up! I dozed off, my abdomen feeling like I'd just cranked out a hundred sit-ups.

As sunset approached, Moose woke us both up. "Opters, get the mosquito netting out. Jelly, get your ass off the ice chests so I can get something to eat."

Jelly rose up onto one elbow—then froze stiffly in place—before *very slowly* lying back down flat on his back. He whispered, "I can't get up right now. I need help. C'mere. Help me. Someone fucking help me!"

Moose bellowed in response: "C'mon Jelly! I'm hungry and I gotta eat something! Get off the fucking ice chests!"

What a charmer.

"S-s-scorpion."

That's when we saw it. A huge scorpion partially nestled in Jelly's belly button, its long tail and fearsome stinger arched menacingly above it.

I was with Jelly on this one. "Don't move! It looks pissed!"

Moose took a slightly different tack. "See what you did, Jelly? Karma is getting you back for all that shit you gave us about being smarter and bringing a cot and all. This is cosmic payback, Mexican style."

Now he's a philosopher?

"What should we do, Moose?" I have no clue where to begin. "Maybe if you stay still, Jelly, he'll crawl back off."

"Nah, you just have to go for it. Tip on your side real quick and he'll roll right off."

Yeah, Moose. Right up until the moment he stabs that warhead into Jelly's flesh to keep his footing.

A minute passed while we all stared at the scorpion. Jelly was sweating like a pig and had gone a little pale. Finally, Moose grabbed a pack of matches from his bag, pulled one free, lit it, and flicked it toward Jelly.

"What the fuck? What are you doing?! You're gonna get him killed!"

Moose didn't say anything, or even look at me. He just removed another match, struck it, and—while it was still flaring into action—dropped it onto Jelly's bare chest.

Talk about forcing the issue!

In the blink of an eye, Jelly lurched to his side and bolted upright. The scorpion fell to the powdery soil; Moose squashed it dead under his sandal, and—without pause—pulled the ice chest out and opened the top. The lingering scent of burnt chest hair, all that remained to mark the moment.

Moose spoke first, albeit with half a tortilla folded into his mouth. "Look, Jelly. Either you were going to get stung or you weren't. I have to eat, and it was time to find out which way it was gonna go down."

Wow. I hope to GOD that I'm never stuck between Moose and food.

Jelly didn't say much of anything the rest of the evening. I'm not sure if he still was sulking over his cot, in a state of shock, or just fearful of sounding weak if he brought it up. Moose and I, on the other hand, couldn't talk about much of anything else. Jelly's taunting ... Moose's noxious fart ... The cot ripping ... Propping up the ruined cot on ice chests ... The scorpion ... The matches ... The quarter-size, hair-free patch of bright red skin that Moose had dubbed, "Jelly's third nipple." We told and retold the story deep into the evening, laughing at the same stupid things over and over.

Could it be that Moose and I were bonding? Becoming pals? GOD, I hope not. I just wanted to be cool. I didn't need to be his buddy, and I certainly had no desire to be "a known associate of a wanted felon."

By midmorning the next day, we were packed and ready for Roberto to come and get us. We sat and sweated under the corrugated tin roof. (It's amazing how the conscious and subconscious mind can affect one's basic bodily functions. None of us ever had the slightest inclination to use the porta potty at camp's edge. We could hold it until we reached the air-conditioned restrooms back at the dealership.) A few hours passed. We were sweating so much I was sure we'd run out of drinkable water by nightfall. Then, what would we do?

Tick-tick-tick-tick, the second hand trudged around the face of my watch. I checked and rechecked; the minutes and hours painfully slow to change. The day dragged on and on. We barely talked to each other, preferring to suffer in silence rather than speak and reveal our concerns.

If I wasn't so miserably hot—and terribly dehydrated by that point—I might actually have teared with emotion the moment Roberto and his beautiful truck returned to deliver us from this hellhole of a campground. Obviously the beneficiary of some fresh tutoring in English, he called out to us, "Hola, my friends! How was your camping?"

"Is my Bus ready?" I shot back, not wanting to dillydally a minute longer in getting back to civilization.

"Si. Está acabado."

"Yes" must not have been included in this morning's English lesson.

We loaded our gear into his truck without needing to be asked and headed back to the dealership. Moose tried to make conversation with Roberto, but the heat, hit-and-miss translations, and bumpy roads conspired to make it impossible to carry on.

You would've thought the 1DRBUS was being put up for sale. It was positively gleaming in the sunlight—parked directly in front of the dealership—as we pulled into the lot. I was in shock at how good it looked. They'd detailed it inside and out, waxed it, cleaned the windows, Armor-Alled the tires, and polished the chrome. About a dozen mechanics, salesmen, lot boys, and office staff stood around it. It was a genuine toss-up as to what was more impressive: my Bus, the gathering, or the inspired look on Roberto's face. His chin up, shoulders back, chest puffed. A moment of honor—in front of his crew and dealership staff—it was amazing. To a man (and two women), they beamed with unambiguous pride to have been of service to us. We hugged and shook hands with every single person there. No one could stop grinning. The language barrier was not an issue. We were all one, of common mission. I think I was literally in shock.

Our bill was just over ninety dollars for everything. Someone from the office produced an old Polaroid camera and we posed for two photographs. The first was of us three gringos and our Bus, the second was of everyone organized into two rows in front of the Bus. Me? I was humbled to my core, a lump in my throat that wouldn't go away. These people had given of themselves unselfishly to help strangers in trouble. It was a pure and genuine kindness—one so foreign to me—and one not easily understood. They *loved* us.

I mailed this postcard to Perro ("Ed Leon") from the VW dealership in La Paz, Baja Sur, Mexico, the day we left for the ferry terminal in Cabo San Lucas. You can see our karmic butt-kicking was well underway: "38 quarts (of oil) to La Paz," "No surfing yet," "Many mosquitos." (The "Ed" at lower left refers to "Moose." Man, could he rip 'em.)

Never drive at night

As we headed south out of La Paz toward Cabo San Lucas that evening, the repeated warnings we'd been given about driving on the highways after dark were on my mind. But, we had lost so much time already that we'd miss yet another ferry departure to the mainland if we didn't press on overnight.

A single, high intensity, off-road spotlight sat atop the spare tire mounted on the front of the 1DRBUS. When it was on, we resembled an oncoming freight train in the darkness. Unfortunately, the regular headlights were so dim, that we couldn't safely drive at a decent speed—and still see far enough in front of us—to avoid something springing forth out of the darkness. So we did the safest thing for *us*. We left the high intensity spotlight on full time. Everyone we encountered flashed their lights, honked, or yelled at us. We were a menace to all, but it was either that, or go slow and miss the ferry. We went from being forever grateful for our treatment at the VW dealership, to being Ugly Americans in less time than it takes to watch a movie. But we pressed on.

The spotlight cast a distinctive and well-defined, wide-angle beam. Panoramic from side to side, it was exceedingly thin top to bottom. To get it to shine far enough down the road to be of any help, the light had to be aimed so it had a crisp, upper "horizon" (level with the bottom of the windshield) and an obscenely bright view of the highway, sandwiched between there and the darkness below the bumper. With every bump or dip in the road, the scene would change with disorienting suddenness, and return to normal just as quickly.

One particularly long stretch of the road cut across a desert landscape transected frequently by seasonal storm washes the Mexicans called arroyos. The road would dip several feet into each of these dry creek beds, run across the bottom, and pop back up onto the desert plain at the other side. With our spotlight often concealing the initial drop until the last instant, it made for some very sudden and unnerving entrances—resulting in us getting some "air time" more than once. During our descent into a wash, the spotlight would point down (literally leaving us in the dark as to what lay more than a few yards ahead) until we reached the bottom and leveled out again. When we exited (running back up the other side), the light would beam mightily into the sky, depriving us a forward view of the road for a few seconds—until we crested the top and resumed level travel.

We'd cycled through about a dozen of these exaggerated whoop-de-dos, when things settled down for a few miles. We began to relax and talk about what we'd been through already. The conversation was dedicated to how crappy everything had gone so far. We griped over breaking down and being delayed. I grumbled about the peasants in Santa Rosalía; people unable, or unwilling, to understand that we were in need of motor oil, even if I *was* saying it all wrong. Moose bitched over missing the first ferry to Puerto Vallarta—and made it abundantly clear there would be hell to pay if we didn't get to the next departure in time. It was hard not to feel impatient over not being at the end of the road already. There was nary a mention of the unfathomable outpouring of affection and support shown us by the people of the dealership. *That gift* we'd experienced mere hours earlier.

Out of nowhere, the road dropped from under us into the deepest wash of all. The spotlight beamed down, rendering us unable to distinguish anything ahead of us for a second or two. Reaching bottom, we leveled out, our horizon of light finally elevated enough to shine forward. A wall of cattle burst out of the darkness—dead ahead. I slammed on the brakes and we began to slide without slowing, directly into the cattle. A hundred pairs of eyes reflected terror. Ghostly illusions, one after another after another, they inexplicably blew past us to one side or the other. The herd parted like Moses's Red Sea, as we skidded through them, our forward speed barely easing on the loose gravel. Thirty, forty, fifty yards. We slid and slid and slid. Abruptly, we reached the other side of the wash and popped up—settling onto level highway again—free of cattle. A completely clear and open highway rose into view before us. It was as if nothing had happened. A hallucination. A bad dream. Launched off a ramp—twenty seconds of chaos and panic—shot back up—and it was done.

Message received. You're but a speck of dust in a cosmic wind. Get over yourselves already.

"We have two of the best..."

Cabo San Lucas was a sleepy little fishing town at the end of the road, and the marina wasn't hard to find. About forty small craft were moored toward one side of the obviously shallow bay. It appeared a major expansion of the small harbor was underway. Two bulldozers pushed piles of rich-looking, red soil into angular hedgerows along the water's edge. A crane repeatedly lowered a big, battered, corroded yellow bucket into the water, before dragging it along a rock jetty that marked the entrance to the man-made port. It didn't seem to be removing much of anything solid from the water, so I guessed it was just dredging up some sand and depositing it along the base of the jetty.

The ferry was a lot bigger than I'd imagined it would be. Though I'd never seen one in real life, I conjectured that cruise ships probably were not much larger than this thing was. All manner of cars, vans, buses, and trucks were lined up on a paved lane alongside the waterfront, each preparing to load into the ship's hold for the overnight crossing to Puerto Vallarta. At the end where the lane neared the front of the ferry, a little finger of a dock jutted out to meet the fully opened, hinged bow of the ship. It was not unlike the jaws of an enormous shark, cocked menacingly skyward, poised to swallow an unsuspecting prey.

We were exhausted from the overnight drive, but relieved to be there with nearly an hour to spare before vehicle load in. We fell in line behind a semi truck and quickly had another big rig roll up behind us. A skinny guy dressed in blue coveralls and carrying several clipboards approached and handed me some papers to fill out. Thankfully, the forms included English translations in brackets below each blank. The usual things you'd expect: make, model, country where registered, plate number, owner's name, type of cargo on board, etc. The agent made it clear that only the driver could remain with the vehicle, so while I filled out the paperwork and waited to load, Moose and Jelly went to the ticket office and bought passage for the three of us and the Bus.

It was a little freaky driving down the ramp and into the cavernous hull of the ship. I guess I'd never thought of it as *tiny*, but the 1DRBUS felt like a child's toy among the buses and trucks. The skinny guy in coveralls waved me forward until the spare tire mounted above my front bumper was literally kissing the ass end of the tractor trailer rig ahead of us. I stayed put in the driver's seat for a bit and the dim light in the ship's hull darkened even further, eclipsed by the Godzilla-proportioned big rig sucking up to my own back bumper. My mirror revealed only a menacingly large VOLVO nameplate spanning my rear window. The distinctive *phsssshat!* of airbrakes engaging memorialized the moment.

Huh ... I didn't know Volvo made trucks. That's reassuring. They probably have good parking brakes.

After a quick last look around the inside of the 1DRBUS to see what was being forgotten, I hopped out and closed the door. Whoops, forgot to leave the keys in the ignition. I kinda wondered about the ALL CAPS insistence of that on the paperwork. I mean, under what circumstances do they need to drive your vehicle off of the boat without you? You didn't complete the trip, but your vehicle did? I best leave that one alone for now.

Stepping back for a better perspective, the 1DRBUS resembled a boxy, Irish cream liqueur tan and root beer brown wheel chock between the two big rigs. I feared its destiny was to absorb the inevitable blow, when one rig or the other broke loose and erased the distance between them.

The route out of the hold was circuitous—and borderline treacherous. The stairs were more like ladders, the passageways narrow and poorly lit. Two flights up, I encountered another of the coverall-clad crewmen, this one going the other direction. The two of us had to turn sideways and square our backs against opposing walls to pass, the space insufficient if one of us had carried a bag or suitcase. The stifling hold reeked of diesel exhaust, tires, and mechanic's grease. Looking up and catching a glimpse of blue sky triggered a physical craving for fresh air.

Once topside, I tracked down the guys at the aft bar. Somehow, they'd already become fast friends with an English-speaking couple on holiday from Sweden, who soon was buying all of the drinks for the five of us. The Swedes didn't have a car below decks. They were traveling as the more typical tourists, via planes, trains, and hired automobiles. I started to tell them about the adventure of loading my Bus down below, but learned quickly: This conversation was to be all about them and the wonders of living in Sweden.

That's okay. They're buying the drinks.

After about an hour, a rumor skittered nervously through the aft deck bar crowd. There was a hurricane somewhere between where we were, and where we were going. It quickly became the exclusive focus of conversation.

"I wonder if the crossing will be cancelled," the female half of the Swedish couple asked.

All eyes turned to Moose for a sign. "Nah, they wouldn't dare. Nut'n to gain by staying here and wasting time."

Yeah Moose. Except for maybe not sinking or drowning. That'd be something to gain by waiting.

The ship's PA system crackled to life, and a man identifying himself as the ship's captain stated he would be addressing us in Spanish, and then repeating everything in English. I understood a word or two during the first announcement, but it was a toss-up as to whether he was saying we were staying put—or was defiantly declaring that nothing would stop us. He wrapped up with a cheerful sounding, "Gracias por su atención."

After a few seconds of dead air, the captain began again, this time in perfect English. "My friends, this is your ship's captain. Many of you, no doubt, have heard the talk of a storm that has recently developed into a hurricane over the ocean west of Puerto Vallarta. Ocean storms are quite typical for this area from late summer into early fall each year, and we are quite familiar with their actions. If you need more to put you at ease, we have just returned from the shipyards in Mazatlán where we have been outfitted with two of the most advanced and powerful diesel engines ever to be utilized on a ship of this size. We have the utmost confidence that we will have no difficulty circumventing the path of the hurricane and arriving in Puerto Vallarta as scheduled. However, we may experience rougher than normal swell activity due to the storm. This poses no danger to passengers or to the ship, but may make a portion of our crossing uncomfortable for those persons susceptible to seasickness. Therefore, if anyone chooses to disembark now and travel on the next ferry, scheduled to depart the day after tomorrow, you are welcome to do so without penalty. Unfortunately for those who have a vehicle on board, it is not possible for us to return it to you at this time. It will be kept in a secure storage lot in Puerto Vallarta until your arrival at the end of the week. All those wishing to disembark now and wait for the next ferry, please identify yourself to a crewman at this time. Thank you for your attention."

"See you guys? Nut'n to worry about," said Moose, breaking into a Cheshire cat grin.

Me? I've got a whole list of things we should worry about! Are you kidding me? We're going to dodge a hurricane in the open ocean? "It may get a little rough"? Sure, I can stay behind if I want, but my car will go ahead to Puerto Vallarta without me? What are the chances Moose and Jelly are going to wait for me in Puerto Vallarta? Shit, I can see myself at the "secure storage lot" now, looking around for the 1DRBUS, which by then will be a thousand miles south, on the beach in La Ticla. Horse shit. There are only lousy alternatives here. Oh well, here goes nothing,

"Sounds great! Let's have another drink and toast the coming adventure."

"Yeah Moose. Let's toast the adventure, ack-ack-ack-ack."

Please Jelly. Not now. This is not the time to play like we're the Three Stooges on a sea cruise. This is insanity, and you know it as well as I do.

We ordered another round, but this time the Swedes declined and said they had to talk alone.

"Well, Opters, looks like this round is on you. You're the one proposing a toast."

Bitchin'. Thanks Jelly.

We did our stupid toast and "clinked" our Styrofoam cups before gulping down our drinks. I was drinking screwdrivers, because other than beer, I didn't really know much else to ask for. The talk soon returned to surfing and the mainland, as the ship's horn sounded and we pushed away from the dock. The huge ship dwarfed anything else in the marina as it eased slowly rearward—toward our exit into the open ocean. The ship's captain apparently wasn't comfortable attempting to turn the enormous ferry around in the narrow channel, so we were going to back all of the way out. Approaching the area where the crane had been dragging the bucket along the edge of the jetty earlier, a strange shudder and dull *thud-thud-thud-thud-thud-thud* reverberated through the guts of the ship below our feet.

"What the fuck was that?" I asked no one in particular.

"Relax, Opters. They're probably just shifting gears."

Yeah, right Moose. New engines and a shitty old transmission. Cap'n probably didn't push the clutch pedal in far enough.

The ship slowed a little, but continued to back out past the end of the jetty. The captain swung us around a full 180—and pointed us due south, into open water—before coming to a dead stop. There seemed to be a lot of scurrying about by crew members with concerned looks on their faces. The engines went quiet. A single, well-defined, dark-black smoke ring rose from the main stack.

"Are we there yet? Ack-ack-ack-ack."

"Yeah, any minute now, Jelly." I had to admit it *was* funny though. Helped to break the tension.

The PA system crackled to life once again, "My friends, this is your captain. It seems the work on the harbor has left an unmarked underwater obstacle in our path. Thankfully, we made only brief and minor contact with the high spot and our inspection has indicated no damage to our ship. Unfortunately, we have determined that it is best to discontinue the use of one of our engines, due to the possibility that one of our propellers was bent slightly when it struck the obstacle. However, you may rest assured that we have full use of the remaining engine and propeller. And because it is one of the most advanced and powerful diesel engines ever to be utilized on a ship of this size, we have confidence that we will experience no further delay in our crossing. Thank you for your attention."

Uh, wait. Didn't you forget the part about the option of waiting for the next ferry? Now we not only have to dodge a hurricane, but do it with only one of the two engines working? Do the Mexican airlines pull this same shit? "Uh, welcome aboard our plane today, ladies and gentlemen. We only have one working engine for this flight, but don't worry because we checked the dipstick last week and it had plenty of oil." I want off.

"Whatsammata, Opters? You look like you saw a ghost?"

"What's the matter?! Are you fucking kidding me? We're doomed. That's what the fuck is the matter! I want off this thing."

Just then, the smoke stack belched a fresh round of black smoke and the remaining workable engine rumbled to life.

"Too late for snivlin', Opters. We're on our way to the mainland. Why don't you have another screwdriver, relax, and enjoy the ride?"

I wish I wasn't so intimidated by him. I'd love to toss Moose overboard right now. I want to throw up, and I don't think it's the screwdrivers.

The two of them walked away and left me to myself—probably their best move right now. I leaned against the railing and looked down at the water. Yep. Only one prop wash coming from the stern. Cabo was sinking into the distance fairly quickly, so maybe we were cruising along okay after all. A few minutes later, only ocean was visible in all directions. A first for me. It brought forth disparate emotions. Yeah, there was a sense of adventure. But foremost, remained a feeling of dread over what may lie before us. The ocean seemed impossibly immense. I pondered how deep it was under us right now.

I'd seen the aftermath of Hurricane Camille in photographs and on television. It had roared ashore between New Orleans and Mobile, Alabama, in 1969. I vividly remember my mom glued to the radio and listening with great interest to the reports, crying because her best friend lived in a small town directly in Camille's path. The friend survived, but her house had been obliterated. Mile after mile, forests full of huge trees were snapped in half. It was as if a huge Weedwacker had passed through, felling the trees like so much tall grass. Piers and boatyards wiped from the Earth. These were the scenes stubbornly residing in my head as I leaned against the railing and watched the sun disappear below the horizon.

I found the guys at a snack counter toward the front of the ship. They each had a plate of shredded pork, rice, and beans, with tortillas at the ready. I got a plate of my own and we ate like we hadn't seen food in a week. We each had a bottle of beer before deciding it was time to call it a night.

Our cabin was just large enough to accommodate two parallel sets of bunks, each attached to an opposing wall. In a corner (as far away as you could get from the doorway) an opening revealed a small closet that held a toilet, a washbasin, and an afterthought of a shower. The shower wouldn't accommodate all of Moose at once, and though skinny enough, I was at least three or four inches too tall for it. Still, it *was* a shower, and none of us had bathed in days. We did our best to clean up and went to bed for the night.

Cabo San Lucas Marina, circa 1978.
They stopped shoehorning gigantic ships like ours
in here a few years later.

Our cursed ferryboat, the *Puerto Vallarta* docked in Cabo San Lucas,
its "shark jaws" front hatch raised, ready to welcome its unsuspecting
fare of trucks, buses, and *us* into its enormous belly.

Moose and Jelly (in the white T-shirts) enjoying "free" drinks, courtesy of our new Swedish friends.

Me, leaving Cabo aboard the ferry.

It seemed like only minutes had passed before two uninterrupted minutes of an obnoxiously loud buzzer—pulsing on and off—awakened us (and, assumedly, everyone else within several miles). The PA system followed, with the captain's voice: "Good evening, my friends. We are sorry to wake you at this late hour. We have been advised that our storm has been given the name of Norman. Norman has unexpectedly intensified into a Category 4 hurricane, but has also changed its course to a little further out to sea. Thankfully, the center of the storm is now forecast to pass approximately seventy miles to the west of our planned route tonight. However, we will be encountering the stronger side of the approaching hurricane, and may have to steer closer to it at times to contend with the large swells and strong winds anticipated in the coming hours. Due to these conditions, we are requiring all persons to remain below decks, and not venture to any exterior or exposed places on this ship—for any reason—until further notified. We believe this restriction will be in effect for several hours. Thank you for your cooperation."

Earlier in the evening, you could feel the ship rise and fall on the swells, but quickly became accustomed to the motion and didn't give it much thought. Now the ship was heaving with a *purpose,* up sharply for a count of six or eight and then freefalling for the same. Hung from a single hook on the back of our cabin door, Moose's wet towel provided an effective measure of how much we were tilting up or down. I guessed the total swing was about fifteen degrees from point to point, and attempted to guesstimate what that angle worked out to, in *feet-of-rise-or-fall* at either end of the ship.

"Hey Jelly, how long do you think this boat is?"

"Why?"

"Because I think I can figure out how big the swells are by using Moose's towel as a plumb bob." *Boy, do I ever sound like*

Poindexter right now. I don't care. I want to know. Besides, I'm feeling a little queasy, and this might take my mind off of it.

"Sure. You do that. I saw a postcard of the ferry in the café. I think it said it was 160 meters long or something like that."

Okay, that'll have to do. Let's see ... 39 inches per meter, divide by 12 ...

"That's a little over 500 feet."

"Shit, Opters. You should've been an astronaut or something."

If only ...

"Thanks, Moose."

Math is easy. Now for the geometry. I hate geometry. I'll need some scratch paper for this part.

"Hey, do you guys know if we are toward the middle of the ship, or closer to one end?"

Blank stares and shoulder shrugs.

"The middle?"

"Thanks Jelly. I'll go with that." Actually, I'm not all that certain it makes a difference. *I hate geometry.*

I multiplied and divided, made crude drawings, scribbled and erased. After several tries, I arrived at the same answer twice.

"Okay, I think if we use the towel to show us the angle of *pitch,* we can more or less figure out how big the swells are out there. In our case, I think the rise and fall of the bow works out to about five feet for every degree of pitch."

"So what does that mean for us, Mr. Wizard? Ack-ack-ack-ack."

"It means that from the lowest part of the trough, to the crest of the next swell, is going to be about five feet; times how many degrees the towel deviates from straight up and down. I'm guessing it's about a fifteen degree swing right now, so that means the swell height is half of five times fifteen, or roughly thirty-seven feet."

"Why half, Opters?"

Smartest thing I've heard Moose say this whole trip.

"Because, like in surfing, you measure the height of a wave from the back, not from the trough in front of it. That's typically about half, so it's what I'm using here."

Right then, we pitched down through a particularly long sequence, and the drop felt like an elevator, but with a long lazy roll to the left included for good measure.

My stomach is not going to last very much longer if this keeps up.

"How big was that one, Opters?"

"I wasn't watching the towel, Jelly" Actually my eyes were closed as I fought back the urge to puke. "Just multiply the degrees by five and divide by two. Or whatever order you want to do it in. The answer is the same. I gotta lie down."

"How do you know the degrees, Opters?"

Must not have taught that in Juvenile Hall...

By now I was clutching my belly and deep breathing to keep from losing my dinner. "Think of it as a La Bella's pizza, Moose." I'm sure that's something he can easily visualize. "The whole pizza is 360 degrees. Cut it into quarters, and each of those is 90 degrees. Cut one of the quarters into 3 pieces and each of those are 30 degrees. Can you take it from there? I'm going to throw up."

I lunged for the toilet at the same time the ship pitched down and listed hard to one side. I landed on hands and knees with my head in the shower. An orange-juice-colored mix of shredded pork, refried beans, and screwdrivers spewed forth, splattering the wall and floor of the tiny shower. Another lurch of the ship answered with another heave, except this time it also shot out of my nose and burned like hell.

"My God, Opters! You gonna be okay?"

"No, I'm fucking dying in here, Moose."

Jelly was next, a few minutes later. He made it to the toilet, but was kneeling across the back of my legs as he hung his head into the bowl. I was too busy heaving to care. After about ten minutes of this, he moaned pitifully and pleaded,

"Dear God, please make this fucking boat stop moving."

I don't think God appreciates you dropping the F-bomb on him, Jelly.

In the wake of a particularly long and gut-wrenching rise, a tantalizingly brief pause at level, and the forward swoon and subsequent rush into the next trough, Moose called out, "I think that one was almost 30 degrees! How big are the swells now, Opters?"

Really Moose? You want me to do math now? I'm puking my guts out. It's all over me. Jelly's barf is on my legs, deposited when he tried to sit up and lost it again. And … you want me to do math?

"Never mind, I'll ask later when you guys are doing better. I'm feeling it now, too; probably because you guys are stinking up the place so bad."

Before I could tell him it worked out to seventy-five-foot seas, I heard our cabin door fly open, with Moose projectile-vomiting into the passageway. Jelly heard it, too, and started laughing, lifting his head from the toilet and snorting so hard that puke bubbled from both nostrils and tears rolled down his cheeks. We were all dreadfully seasick. The seas were getting rougher and the rise and falls were joined frequently by some serious side to side rolling action.

I wonder if you can die from seasickness. Or maybe you just feel like you are going to—so you jump overboard to end it quicker?

This is your captain speaking: "We have the utmost confidence we will
have no difficulty circumventing the path of the hurricane and arrive
in Puerto Vallarta as scheduled. However, we may experience rougher
than normal swell activity due to the storm."

It went on for hours. Eventually, I was able to partially
stand in the shower by bracing my elbows against the sides,
pressing my knees forward against one wall and arching my
back against the other. When I was pretty sure I could maintain
this pose, I turned the water on, hoping to rinse some of our
combined vomit from me. The spray diluted the minimally
digested broth, but only about half of it was making it down
the drain, causing the water to back up. I tried to mash the
more stubborn pieces underfoot and shepherd them through
the grate with my toes.

The ship rolled so far over once, I thought for sure we were
going to capsize. Without warning, a big gush of nasty: vomit,
toilet tissue, and feces-laden water erupted from both toilet and
shower, dislodging the drain grate along with it. Something

had failed in the ship's sewer system. Its contents sloshed to and fro in the wastewater holding tanks, only slightly trailing the rhythm of the rolling and pitching of the ship.

Already wearing much of his own dinner, Moose came dragging back into the cabin from the passageway. He made it to the bathroom entrance, only to be met with an ankle-deep stew of sewer sludge—racing to greet him like the incoming tide on a beach. No pristine whitewater here, though. Like his namesake having been mortally wounded by a hunter's bullet, he bellowed, turned, slipped, and fell to the floor, in a vain attempt to dodge the inevitable.

All three of us. Stricken brethren. As reduced and humiliated as someone can be… short of death.

"Maybe we should've waited for the next ferry."

Not quite the Stooge Cruise you hoped for, eh, Jelly?

CHAPTER 7

THE MAINLAND

Batman in the jungle

The ferry eventually made it to Puerto Vallarta. A warm and cloudless afternoon, a gentle breeze, and gorgeous landscapes greeted us. The advertised, fourteen-hour crossing had lasted twenty-six, but felt every bit of a hundred and twenty-six. We managed to wash ourselves and rinse our clothes out pretty well, but it was impossible to get our shoes completely dry. Just too damn humid. We never did eat another meal on the ship, nor drink anything other than soda pop. We were too weak to care about much of anything—except for getting off that God-forsaken boat.

I finally steered the 1DRBUS out of the ship's hold at dusk, and we departed the ferry landing. Once again we'd been delayed. *Yet again*, we were running *counter* to the daylight. We stopped just before leaving town to eat, and the meal seemed to give us a second wind. We decided to go ahead and drive for as long as we could manage, camp until sunrise, and then continue south.

The road from Puerto Vallarta winds through some dense tropical jungle as you get farther south. Several stretches of vegetation are so heavy and full you are driving in a damp, dark, and drizzly tunnel, day or night. After sundown, it can be absolutely devoid of light, and not just a little bit spooky. Bats, rats, skunks, and toads provide the only glimpses of animal life.

Confident in our freshly rebuilt engine, we blew down the road at a pretty good clip. The air, sodden beyond capacity, rendered it mandatory to keep the wipers going full tilt, just to track the white line splitting the road in front of us. Our high-intensity, off-road spotlight, once again thrown into action, illuminated the bats that swooped low enough (into the beam in front of us) before they vanished into the dark mist above.

We had Led Zeppelin's *"Dazed and Confused"* cranking full blast—the opening bass notes strained the subwoofer, vibrated the windows, and overloaded our senses:

Ba doo-doo-doo-doo. Ba doo-doo-doo-doo …

Something wasn't sounding quite right with the stereo. I detected a weird humming or groaning noise, a constant and unrelenting, near-subliminal *moaning*. I punched the pause button on the cassette player, and the strange sound didn't go quiet with the music. You couldn't tell where the wailing was coming from, but you could feel it on your skin and in your gut. It enveloped you.

Waaaoooohhmmmmmmm … Waaaoooohhmmmmmmm …

It was otherworldly—and creepy to the core.

"What *now*, Opters?"

"I don't know, Moose."

Reflexively, I eased my foot off of the gas pedal, and the 1DRBUS began to slow. We all exchanged worried but puzzled looks. The, *Waaaoooohhmmmmmmm ...* gradually faded, until it went away altogether.

"Okay, that was weird. I have no idea what it could've been, but it's gone now. Let's leave the stereo off for a bit."

Transaxle? It's the only thing I can think of that could conceivably throw off a sound like that ... *I guess ... hell, I don't know ...*

We drove on, and after three or four minutes without consequence, I pressed "play," and Robert Plant's melancholy vocals filled the night again. On cue, just as he led into a long instrumental with, *"was created below ..."*

Waaaoooohhmmmmmmm ... Waaaoooohhmmmmmmm ...

Fuck. There it was again,

Waaaoooohhmmmmmmm ... Waaaoooohhmmmmmmm ...

Again I hit the pause button, and ease off the gas. The wailing faded into the night once more.

"I'm going to leave the tunes off for a bit, you guys."

"Whatever you say, Opters. That noise is freaking me out."

"Me too, Moose." *It's not enough that we're driving in a mist-laden, jungle-shrouded tunnel, bats swooping and darting in and out of our path. The jungle is moaning at us, too?*

I didn't know who or what was haunting us right then, but that noise messed with our heads big time. I got back up to speed, listening hard for the transaxle to act up. Sure enough, at fifty-eight or fifty-nine miles an hour, the pitiful, quavering moan kicked on again.

Waaaoooohhmmmmmmm ... Waaaoooohhmmmmmmm ...

This time, without the added fervor of *"Dazed and Confused"* pumping through us, the source of the sound was traced to the fresh-air vents on the ceiling over the front seats. Old "Splitties" (pre-1968, split-window VW Buses) have an "eyebrow" that extends out over the top of the windshield a few inches. The bottom surface has screened openings that route fresh air from *outside* the windshield, into a louvered ventilation box on the ceiling *inside* the windshield. A lever opens and closes it; a turn of a knob directs the air flow straight back, or to the sides. The heavy mist had been coursing through the box for over an hour—leaving behind small droplets of moisture along the way—until it partially was filled with water. At just the right speed, the air blowing over the puddle of water inside the box was strumming exactly like when you put your lips to a half-filled soda bottle and blow across its opening. More or less liquid, or vary the air flow, and you change the pitch.

The sheet metal box was amplifying and disseminating the sound via the ceiling in a way that made it seem possible that you yourself might be the source. Each time that ventilation box began its distant thundering, I'd unconsciously react by easing off of the gas pedal and slowing down. Hence, the vibrations would lessen, and then cease altogether as the volume of air flowing across the puddle in the ventilation box fell below the threshold necessary to thrum. Resume the perfect speed, and, *Waaaoooohhmmmmmmm* ... returned. Once we had figured it out, I swerved from side to side a couple of times, spilling enough water from the box to quiet the drumming. So what, if our laps got a little wet? The creepy wailing was solved.

We had a good laugh and kidded one another for a few minutes over being freaked out by the mysterious sound—although you could hardly blame us. We were on a dark, drizzly, and deserted road populated only by nocturnal vermin, with an overgrown jungle completely blocking out the sky above. *This* was the stuff of horror movies.

I reached for the "play" button, but didn't make it before, *BLAM!* A bat blasted out of the darkness—and, like a freakishly large moth—splattered against the driver's half of the split windshield. Badly broken, but intact and now spread-eagled, it was immediately captured by the wiper blade sliding over the mess, pinning it against the glass. Bloody streaks, smearing in scarlet arcs, spanned my field of view. Wipers on full speed, the spectacle unrelentingly cycles: left-right-left-right-left-right, absent only a bloodcurdling scream to complete the scene. My left foot stabbed the clutch pedal to the floor, my right flew from gas to brake. Our tires squealed, sixty-five to a dead stop, straddling the centerline of the narrow two-lane road.

Jelly yelled, "Turn off the wipers! Maybe it'll get free!"

"Its brains are splattered all over the fucking windshield! It's not going anywhere on its own."

If my eyes could open any wider right now, they'd overrun my eyebrows.

"Get it off of there!" Moose was freaking out. "What the fuck happened? How'd you manage to hit a fucking bat? Don't they have *radar* or something?"

"Yes, they have fucking radar! They never run into anything. It's impossible!" *At least that's what all the books say. How could this be?*

"Well, I don't care why you hit it! Get out there and get it the fuck off the window. Jeez! This trip is already cursed, and you have to go and kill a fucking Vampire Bat?"

Now it's a Vampire *Bat?*

Totally creeped out, I slowly opened my door and leaned out my head a bit. I looked to the rear, scanning the pitch-black jungle, girding for a demon to spring from the darkness. Afraid to just step right out and take care of business, I hugged the door to my chest, using it as a shield and triple checking my surroundings—up, down, left, right ... repeat. One foot slowly extended to the pavement—one last check of the jungle behind us—before lowering my second foot. Jelly reached over and jabbed a finger into my exposed arm pit, thinking it was funny. In my panic, my forehead banged hard against the top of the door jamb, my shorts got caught on the latch, and I scraped the crap out of my elbow, diving headfirst back into my seat.

"Whatsammata, Opters? See a ghost? Ack-ack-ack-ack …" Jelly was laughing hysterically, but not Moose.

"Quit fucking around and let him get the bat off of there, Jelly! This isn't funny!"

So I slinked out as carefully as possible and lifted the wiper arm from the bat. Unfortunately, the bat was so wrapped around the blade, it wouldn't fall free on its own. Drawing upon residual adrenaline—from Jelly scaring the shit out of me—I grasped a blood-soaked wing and pulled the poor creature free. It slipped from my fingers and onto the roadway at my feet. Without thinking, I wiped my hand across the belly of my T-shirt, anxious to be rid of the dead bat's bodily fluids. The image of Dan-O wiping snot on his sleeve hit me. Fuck it. The bat's history and we were underway again.

We were quiet for a minute before Moose asked in a solemn tone: "What do you think you guys? Are we fucked? That has to be some kind of omen, right?"

Slack-jawed, and in awe of his child-like acknowledgement of the possibility of kismet, I turned to face him,

"Uh, Yeah Moose. Like the town going dark at breakfast our first night? The eight-hundred-mile oil leak? The only part we needed to fix it, missing from an unopened 'Complete Set of VW Engine Seals' master pack? A hundred cows across our path in the dry wash? The ferry running aground in Cabo? Hurricane-fucking-Norman?!! Which omen did I miss, Moose?"

"Don't fret, Moose. We're on our way to paradise, right, Opters?"

Or hell. Right now, I'm not too sure which it will be.

"Hey, I say we keep going as long as we can tonight. I'm too freaked out to sleep now anyway. It'll be light in a couple more hours and we can decide then what's next, okay?"

I mean, what are we going to do? Turn around and go home? Camp here in hell's jungle? I don't fucking think so.

A handful of warm ice cream

The sun had been up for an hour by the time we rolled into the first village established enough to have its own PEMEX station. A trucker pulled up and climbed out of his rig, evidently to stretch his legs and get some coffee. He appeared to be Anglo, so I said,

"Good morning."

"Good morning! How're you guys doing? Heading north or south?"

"South. A ways past Tecomán to a surf spot called La Ticla."

"You know the bridge isn't finished over the Ostula River before there, right? I mean it was, but now it's not. Washed out again about a month ago. Third time they've tried to get the highway across that spot, and the third time it's washed out. It's a bitch, because it'd save me a shitload of driving to go straight through to Acapulco instead of over more damn mountains."

"Wow. So you drive this route all the time?"

"Yep. Acapulco–Puerto Vallarta, Puerto Vallarta–Acapulco. Heading back up to Puerto today. Waited overnight down the road a bit. I never do this last stretch in the dark. Too dangerous. The Mexicans call it Selva de Cuitzmala, the 'Jungle Cuitzmala.' I call it 'hell on earth.'"

"Yeah, we drove down through there last night. Creepy place. What does 'cootie-mala' mean?"

"Keets-mawla. I'm pretty sure it means 'trouble' or 'worry' or something akin to that."

"So, the 'Jungle of Trouble' would be close?"

"Well if not exact, it's close enough. That jungle is bad news. Nothing good ever happens in there. There are tribes of Indians in that jungle that still believe in witchdoctors and black magic and shit. Don't go through there at night again. You probably got lucky."

"Okay … thanks, I think."

"De nada." The trucker saw my puzzled look and added, "De nada. It means something like, 'no worries' in Spanish. You're gonna need that."

More than a little freaked out, I decided it was best to keep the trucker's story to myself for now. I'll save it for a night when we are sitting around a fire on the beach in La Ticla.

The highway took us around the east side of the bustling coastal city of Manzanillo. I'm pretty sure it would be fun to spend a day or two there exploring, but we motored on by. We pressed on until we reached Tecomán, the last actual city before La Ticla. The road was far from dull. Stretches of it veered off onto rough patches every few miles, before returning to the smooth new asphalt of the Trans-Coastal Highway the Mexicans were building. Little pop-up villages dotted the route, apparently in support of the road construction crews. Each had a few small shops, and a dirt lot holding an odd assortment of materials and equipment. The most conspicuous place in each of the tiny villages was a cantina. Although it was an early weekday morning, every one of them we passed had at least a few men out front, holding beer bottles. Of all ages, it's hard to say if the men were leftovers from the night before, or were getting primed to start the new workday.

We passed the occasional large ranch on the outskirts of Puerto Vallarta, and then again along the fringes of

Manzanillo, opulent estates that would be conspicuous in the wealthiest of enclaves in California. In stark contrast to these, the majority of the people we saw were miserably poor. Sure, the city centers had a handful of families that might be considered middle class, but once you were away from town, squalor and surrender were everywhere.

We rolled into Tecomán in the afternoon, and the main boulevard bustled with activity. It was a classic, small Mexican city, with a large town square anchored prominently by a huge Catholic Church building (or should I say, "castle?") These monoliths were enormous in relation to everything else in most towns. The tallest and most architecturally ornate buildings you could imagine, standing watch over peasant and passersby alike. A constant reminder of who had organized (conquered) a random collection of indigenous Indian tribes into a semi-functioning, heavily stratified society.

We went straight to an *agua-purificada* dispensary and filled every container we had with water we could trust, since Moose had said the water in La Ticla could be, as he put it, "a little sketchy." For the first time since we'd crossed the U.S.– Mexico border a week ago, the three of us walked around for a bit to see the sights and soak up some of the local atmosphere. We ducked in and out of the small shops lining the Market District. Not the type of tourist traps filled with useless crap that you find in Tijuana. These were actual stores, catering to the local population. We bought fresh bananas, guavas, papayas, and something called *papausa*. We bought only one of those, despite the clerk swearing it was wonderful. It looked like a mutant gray-green cantaloupe covered in irregular lumps, and it had a gaping crack in it, revealing a mushy-wet pink flesh inside. Moose tasted it first. He didn't say if it was good or not, but dug two fingers back into the crack, scooping out a second load of pink mush and licking his hand clean.

He could say whatever he wanted about it now. Watching his slobber-slickened fingers dig back in, killed any chance of me trying a bite.

"Fuck, Moose! Way to ruin it for the rest of us."

At least Jelly wasn't going in for sloppy seconds.

Moose flashed a mouth-half-open goofy smile, showing enough of the pink mush coating his teeth and tongue to verify he was loving it. "Git your own! This is killer. Like eating warm ice cream."

We both passed on getting more papausa, but Jelly did go back for two big sacks of limes.

I swear. Dude has a lime fetish or something.

I asked him, "What are all the limes for Jelly?"

"They're for making ceviche. Raw fish, onions, tomatoes, and peppers soaked in lime juice for a couple of days. Ain't you ever heard of ceviche?"

Spraying us both with pink spittle, Moose chimed in, "Git on, Chef Jelly! Opters, Jelly makes the best ceviche in the world, and I'm gonna sling me some fish in El Faro to make it with."

I'd ask where El Faro is, but "fish" and "faro" were the preeminent spittle-slingers.

All the right moves

Loaded full of fuel, food, and water, and an hour more daylight remaining than we'd need to get there, we hit the road for the final jaunt to La Ticla. We were feeling pretty giddy now, excited to be so near to "Paradise." Moose insisted on riding shotgun. He was bouncing up and down in his seat like a preschooler, constantly pointing out one thing or another to us. The two-lane highway was newly completed on this stretch. We were making great time, heading southeast and playing peekaboo with the ocean. We weaved through overgrown hillsides and a few spotty agricultural areas, each no more than a mile across. A series of curves bended the road almost 180 degrees away from the coast, taking us inland, away from where we were headed.

"Woo-hoo! Almost there! Just a couple more miles to the turn off now! Yeeaaaaaahhhhh!!!"

The echo of Moose's guttural yell barely faded, we were met with a barricade across the road. A half sheet of weathered plywood bore a large, black, spray-painted arrow, pointing to a heavily rutted dirt road off the side of the highway. This wasn't at all reminiscent of the on-and-off stretches of half-built road we had encountered up this point. More like an emergency, "oh shit" kind of detour.

"I don't remember this part. Let's take the exit and see if it gets us across the river."

Yeah Moose, if the bridge across the river is anything like this piece of shit, pack-mule trail, we should be on the other side in no time.

The dirt road took us straight down a hill, turned to follow an embankment for a hundred yards or so, and then dead-ended in a dirt lot holding an assortment of parked bulldozers and dump trucks. Two official looking men wearing hardhats and orange vests motioned us over to them.

"El camino está cerrado aquí." ("The road is closed here.")

"What are they saying, Moose?"

"They said the bridge isn't finished, but the trucks are crossing the river just fine, and we should make it without any problem, too."

Wow. English makes things so complicated. They said all that in like, five words.

"Great! Ask 'em where we should cross."

Poor Moose. "Qué dondé está mejor location to vamanos otra side? Neccesita yo y mi dos amigos cruzar La Ticla. ¿Por dónde pasan los camiones grandes?

That even sounded tortured to me.

"Tu coche es demasiado pequeño. No lo logrará. Pero si quieres ver dónde se cruzan los camiones, gira a la izquierda y mira por ti mismo." ("Your car is much too small. It won't make it. But if you want to see where the trucks are crossing, turn to the left here and look for yourself.")

"What'd he say, Moose?

"He said that we can cruise across with the trucks down there to the left a bit."

"Oh man, that's cool. I thought we were screwed. Let's go!"

With that, we turned to the left, went another hundred yards or so, and got our first clear view of the Ostula River. Despite being the principal drainage for a large agricultural area, ringed by 3,500-foot mountains 20 miles to our east, it wasn't really what I would call a river. More like a muddy wash about 60 yards wide, running down the middle of a rock and boulder-strewn arroyo that had to be at least 150 yards from bank to bank. There was an assortment of old, beaten-down field trucks on the opposite side, lined up and awaiting the okay to cross. A big flatbed, with a half load of wooden produce crates pulled forward, tapped his horn and waved to a group of people who were gathered off to the side of the staging area. Fifteen or twenty people ran and climbed into the back of the truck, many of them carrying bags or packs and such. Once loaded with all he could carry, the truck gingerly pressed forward into the rocky arroyo. The driver worked hard at steering around the largest of the rocks and ruts, but some evidently were unavoidable. More than once, it was a death-grip hold of the side boards that kept passengers from making an unscheduled exit from the back of the truck.

I studied his path and the way he attacked the route.

Must avoid the large boulders. Watch out for the spots where the water was obviously deeper. Try your best to maintain a constant speed and absolutely, positively, never stop moving, lest you get stuck.

We watched another crossing, nearly identical to the first. Only this time, the driver *did* stop—following a particularly violent lurch—and couldn't get the truck moving again. He yelled to the people in the back of his truck. The entire group jumped down and helped to push the truck free. Some were outwardly miffed once it had resumed the crossing, when the driver kept going and they had to make it the rest of the way on their own.

"You got this, Opters?" said Jelly, sounding more than a little nervous.

"Sure he's got it, Jelly. This is the Wonderbus. Right, Opters?"

I'd been called out. Even during the struggle through the Baja desert, I'd been talking smack about the 1DRBUS. Now I had no choice but to go for it.

"No problema." *I just had to memorize the route and not stop, no matter what.*

We watched one more truck successfully navigate the route, before deciding it was time to go for it. I revved the engine and gave the horn a couple of quick toots to let the other side know it was our turn to cross. The last thing we needed was to meet a big-ass truck full of people, smack-dab in the middle of the river!

Rolling down into the arroyo brought on a torrent of thoughts and emotions. All the ones anyone would expect to have, with pole position belonging to: *"What the fuck am I doing?"* But also present was a feeling of calm, single-minded determination, and pride. I was going to *do* this thing. My mom would say I *shouldn't*. My dad, I *couldn't*. Fuck him. I'm doing it.

We slogged across. It was amazing. I felt like a fighter pilot outmaneuvering anti-aircraft flak bursts. All the right moves, only dipping into a hazard long enough to bypass a more treacherous one beside it. Pushing through roiling patches of water deep enough to hide all four tires from view. Hah! We were out the other side, greeted by hoots, hollers and several loud blasts of truck horns.

Me. I did that. Paul E. Opters had pulled it off. My chest was puffed and my smile broad. *Thank you, God!*

Now that we were on dry land, it occurred to me that we'd have to reprise the crossing to leave. Oh well. Not the time to worry about that now. We've got at least six weeks here— or as long as we can make do with what water we have. We may have to consider brushing our teeth with beer or tequila, though. The three of us were pumping our fists and cheering as we made the final turn toward town a couple of hundred yards down the muddy road. We were in La Ticla. *Hallelujah!*

Heading west toward the beach, via the main boulevard through beautiful downtown La Ticla.

CHAPTER 8

THE PROMISED LAND

Living in paradise

It was every bit as beautiful and untouched as Moose had built it up to be. A sparkling blue seashore, graced with line upon line of long, perfect waves, the spray blowing back off of their crests, catching the sunlight as they broke. A wide, flat sandy beach gracefully curved around the shoreline for as far as you could see—north *and* south. Dense groves of tall, slender coconut palm trees were everywhere. Tropical birds waded in the shallows of a shimmering pond; formed when a sandbar rose across the mouth of the Ostula River. Large mounds—each a blend of graying palm fronds, coconuts and twisted driftwood—peppered the beach, looking like they'd never been touched.

We pulled up to our new home, a rickety old bamboo-and-palm-frond shelter that the Mexicans called a *palapa*. It was neatly tucked into the edge of a coconut palm grove, on a little spit of sand separating the Pacific Ocean end of the river from the beaches to the north.

No people; not in the surf, nor on the beach. In fact, after we'd crossed the wash and driven through "downtown" La Ticla, we spotted only a small handful of villagers, and most of those were peeking out at us from the doorways to their crude huts. Their physical stature strikingly less than even the average Mexican. They came across as shy and worried.

The beachfront in La Ticla. Our camp was under
the coconut palms to the right.

What a cruel dichotomy, I thought. Here they are—immersed in a tropical splendor most only fantasize about, but living in one room huts without electricity, clean water, or indoor plumbing. Subsisting on a diet so devoid of proper nutrition, they appeared destined to remain a universally, diminutive people. The world had passed them by until now, but that was about to change. The coming of the new highway would quickly render the familiar unrecognizable. The tiny trickle of travelers soon would be a flood. And it was scaring the hell out of them.

Not so terribly unlike them, we were here to experience their hidden paradise before completion of the highway would irrevocably expose it to the world. I understood now why Moose wouldn't tolerate stopping to surf anywhere else along the way, always in such a damn hurry. We likely would be the last trio of gringo surfers to have this place completely to ourselves. Forever.

All of the animals, save one, walked in and out of the homes in La Ticla as they pleased. They drew the line at burros.

Where's the surf?

It was nearly dark by the time we had fully situated ourselves under the palapa. Moose and Jelly restored a partially dismantled river-rock fire ring, and I collected enough dry driftwood to get a nice fire going. I pulled the 1DRBUS in close enough for the passenger side barn doors to open into the hut. I made up my bed in the Bus, the guys under the palapa. We were beyond exhausted, and it felt good.

Moose was up first the next morning, stirring the coals left by last night's fire, trying to revive it enough to make some coffee. We had a clear view of the ocean from the palapa, but not the surf. It was cracking and rumbling most of the night, but nary a whisper this morning.

"Hey Moose. How do the waves look?"

"I don't know. I'm busy making coffee, Jelly. Get your ass out of bed and go look."

Jelly walked out to a little rise of sand between us and the ocean. He stood there for several minutes, spying in all directions before looking down, slowly shaking his head like he'd lost a can't miss bet.

"There's nothing, Moose. Not a ripple. I've never seen *anywhere* so flat as here."

"C'mon. Grab your board and we'll paddle out. Opters, you too."

"What for? It's flat. No waves. Are you sure this is the right place?"

"You saw it last night. Sets as far as you could see. *Of course*, this is the place."

The three of us stood on the berm and watched for a half hour. The biggest wave we saw wouldn't get your knees wet. It was pathetic.

"The tide's all wrong. That's okay, it'll get good later."

Right Moose. Today "later", or next week "later"?

"Let's eat." There it was. In order of importance: Surf, eat, get stoned, surf, eat, nap, repeat.

Actually, it didn't bother me much to see the surf flat that first morning. I'd been hiding my concerns we'd be greeted with huge waves. Waves that were *way* beyond my confidence level and I'd have to make a choice: Gut it out or sit it out. At least this way, maybe I'd have the chance to work my way up to the challenges ahead.

We spent the day exploring the area for a couple of miles around us. We came upon a huge sea turtle upended near the shoreline, struggling feebly to right itself. I said we should do something to help it, but Moose was adamant we didn't intervene. He explained the natives had stranded it like that so it would die, and later they'd make soup with its meat. It seemed so sad, but we agreed it probably was a worse idea to piss off the locals by helping the turtle escape. I thought back to the tiny stature of the people we'd seen peeking out of the huts yesterday.

With fish, pigs, chickens, and now turtle on their menu, why did they look so malnourished? Or maybe we were just overgrown, and they represent what God intended? All questions for another time …

One of the dozens of sea turtles we saw on the beaches of La Ticla.

The surf was flat for three days before it finally was worth paddling out. We hung around the camp a lot. Moose made friends with a local named Miguel on the road construction crew who sold him some pot, and he traded a few of his dirty magazines to another guy in exchange for a bottle of authentic, locally crafted mezcal, replete with a grizzled worm at the bottom.

We hiked south down the beach a way to check things out, and came upon the same sea turtle we'd seen inverted on the beach three days earlier. Far from showing any sign of life, two of its legs were oozing stubs, flies swarmed the rotting carcass. No one had come to lay claim since we first spotted it. What a *horrible* waste. We'd had the chance to save it, and I felt really bad for letting things play out as they had. Moose said some kids had no doubt flipped the turtle on its back just for something to do, never having any intention of retrieving it for food. Opportunistic dogs, or wild pigs had probably chewed off the poor thing's feet, likely while it was still alive.

Man, this place is unforgiving.

The thought crossed my mind that we could die here and no one would ever know of it—or find our bodies. It may as well be another planet.

We tried the mezcal that night. Its smell reminded me of paint thinner, and it burned like it going down. The second and third sips weren't any better. Moose said it was a special blend, a concoction that included peyote cactus—and that it was more of a drug, than a drink. *Oh well, when in Mexico ...*

What a mistake. After a shot and a half of the stuff, I was done. Not drunk, but intoxicated in a way I'd never experienced before. The shadows cast by our fire gyrated helter-skelter on the curtain of jungle foliage that surrounded us. I did a double take on the smoke to make sure it actually was *rising*, not *returning* to be consumed by our fire. Psychedelics I had tried in college had nothing on this stuff. Moose conducted an imaginary orchestra with a burning stick. Lingering trails of yellow, red, and orange were left hanging in the air.

If this magical elixir is the choice of the locals, it's no wonder the bridge won't stay up, and that poor sea turtle was forgotten. They're tripping their asses off on this shit.

Sure, I'd had tequila with a worm at the bottom of the bottle in the past. Strong, but no big deal. This stuff had to have come from the same peyote cactus and process that produced the drug, mescaline. It was LSD in a bottle.

We all were unconscious within an hour. Dead to the world. Passed out on top of bedrolls. Way too high to get under the covers before succumbing to the worm.

"Estos son muy peligrosos!"

A headache awakened me before the sunrise did the next morning. Water. I had to have water. I craved it like Moose pursued food. Our campsite was a mess. Whoever it was that had a party here last night didn't bother to pick up after themselves. Thankfully, the surf was flat again, so we stayed in bed past noon.

"Let's go sling some fish in El Faro."

"In the ocean, Moose?" *Yeah, it sounded that stupid as it passed my lips.*

"Of course, in the ocean, Opters! That's where they keep the fish here. Ack-ack-ack-ack."

Thanks, Jelly.

Moose, making sure this is the road that takes us to El Faro.

Paul Wilson

"Midway Rest Area," along the La Ticla to El Faro road.
(Now a modern highway.)

We gathered up the Hawaiian sling, our fins, masks, and snorkels and drove south—aboard the 1DRBUS—down the road to El Faro. Calling it a "road" was being generous. It was closer to twin, parallel footpaths than an actual road, rising and falling through a series of sharp little hills, gullies, and random turns, much like the kiddie roller-coaster at a carnival. It was muddy and badly rutted in spots, *especially* on the hills. A running start was required to make it up some of the rises. The downhill runs were more of a controlled skid, as we tried our best to stay out of the bushes on either side. Several times, as we neared El Faro, the twin furrows would dissolve onto the beach for a few hundred, driftwood-delineated yards, before ducking back up into the jungle. The hour it took to navigate the dozen or so miles to El Faro was like being on a jungle safari, and loads of fun. The trail led us down onto the pristine, white-sand beach of a small cove that was encircled by a near-shore, underwater reef. A picket fence of islets, extending from a rocky point to the south, blocked all but the largest of surges instilled by the ocean swells, the water clear, calm, and beckoning. Moose let us know we'd arrived.

A wide spot in La Ticla–El Faro "highway."
(I believe that's the mayor's house on the left.)

We snorkeled for a couple of hours, each trying our hand with the Hawaiian sling. I came up empty, despite letting it fly in the general direction of a few large fish. Moose and Jelly each managed to nail a couple, so we knew our dinner this evening would be fish. We just didn't know what *type* of fish they were.

Late in the day, dark clouds began rolling in from the south. Along with the clouds, a small, flat-bottomed fishing boat the locals called a *panga*, motored into the cove and stopped just short of the beach. One of the two men aboard jumped into the waist-deep water and worked to untie something they'd lashed to the side of the boat. When it had been pulled free, the panga was beached, and the two of them proceeded to haul a huge shark, tail first, half onto the sand. At about ten to twelve feet, the shark was only a bit shorter than the boat, and it sported a chest as thick as a cow's.

"What kind of shark is that, Moose?"

"I don't know. How about you, Mr. Wizard? Do you know?"

"Not a clue, except it's fucking big!" *And hopefully not the kind that eats people ...*

One of the fishermen jogged off, reappearing ten minutes later behind the wheel of an old beater pickup truck. The five of us did our best to wrestle the beast into the back, but it was much too long and heavy, leaving the enormous tail fin to drag along the ground. They tied the panga upside-down on top of the shark, and made ready to leave. The wind was beginning to come up, and the clouds were rapidly growing darker, but we decided to follow the fishermen and their prize into El Faro proper, before getting on our way back to La Ticla.

Young kids, boys mostly, came from all directions to excitedly run alongside the shark when we reached the village. The pickup pulled up and parked next to some other fishermen who were stacking and covering their gear for the night. We watched as six men struggled to drag the shark from the truck onto a tattered blue tarp not quite big enough to hold both the head and tail at the same time.

Flash ... *KABOOM!* A sudden bolt of lightning and near instantaneous crack of thunder startled us all.

I didn't think we should stick around any longer, and made that clear,

"Shit. Sure looks like it's gonna dump. We'd better get on the road now, or it will be too muddy to make it back." *The 1DRBUS may have superpowers, but mud is mud.*

We motioned to the fishermen we were going to leave, just as another flash ... *KABOOM!* ... went off, this one closer than the first.

One of the original men who caught the shark called to us. "La tormenta hara qué el camino sea intransitable está noche. Estaras atrapado en el barro antes de llegar lejos." ("The storm will make the road impassable tonight. You'll be stuck in the mud before you get far.")

"What'd he say, Moose?" *I don't think the translation this time is, "No worries, everything is fine."*

"He said the storm is here and the road will be too muddy to pass ... *Something* like that."

Another flash ... *KABOOM!* Rain started falling.

"I hate to say it guys, I think he's probably right. We barely made a few of those hills as it was. Any more mud and we're stuck bigger than shit." *I picture spending the night axle-deep in a watery bog, Moose peeing out a window to avoid stepping outside. Nah. Let's stay somewhere around here for now.*

"Por favor, quédense. Tengo un cobertizo en el que estarán a salvo esta noche."

Moose translated for us, "He invited us to stay at his farm tonight."

Flash ... *KABOOM!* Flash ... *KABOOM!*

Okay God. We got the message already.

The fisherman looked anxious and gestured for us to follow him, "¡Debemos irnos ahora!"

The rain *really* began to come down, and I didn't need Moose to help with this one. "Get in! We gotta go now! We're gonna follow him!"

It was only a mile or two, but you could sense that even *this* short distance soon would be impassable if this downpour kept up much longer. He led us to a small, white-and-rust-colored, corrugated tin shed nestled in a small clearing at the edge of untamed jungle. A bamboo-and-palm-frond shelter extended over a quasi-carport nearest the road. The fisherman went in, lit an old lantern, and waved us in behind him. No larger than twelve by twelve feet inside, with a slanted roof about seven feet above the bare ground, it wasn't much to look at. The roar of wind and unrelenting clatter of rain against tin was unnerving.

The fisherman methodically moved his lantern up and down, walking slowly along each wall, carefully inspecting the inside of the shed. He spotted a large scorpion scurrying for cover and quickly crushed it under his sandal. A mud hornet's nest the size of a grapefruit clung to an ancient wooden beam over the doorway. With a card-shark's sleight of hand and a magician's flair, he snapped the blue bandana from his neck, enshrouded the nest, and spun it free from its roost in a single motion. Instantly, the fury of the angry hive eclipsed the racket of the storm outside. Ten fingers snatched four corners of fabric, his pinkies twirling the deadly purse closed.

Is it my imagination, or is the bundle gyrating under the coordinated efforts of the swarm? Lord help us if they make a break for it.

He held the bandana at arm's length, maneuvered downwind twenty or thirty yards into the darkness, stopped in his tracks, and made ready. A flash of lightning backlit his sorcerer's pose as he tossed the hive, spun on his heels, and ran like hell back to the shed. The gusting wind quickly dispersed the furious swarm and kept them from overtaking him *or* returning to the shed.

Back inside, he didn't miss a beat and returned to scanning the interior carefully. With a start, he recoiled from something in the corner near the floor and backed away toward the door. The harsh light from the lantern exaggerated the look on his face.

He spoke excitedly: ¡Quédense atrás! ¡Estas son muy peligrosas! ¡Espero que sólo haya una! ("Stay back! These are very dangerous! I hope there is only this one!")

He picked up a dried, splintering piece of bamboo, stripped off a suitable skewer, crept close to the critter, and speared at it until it was safely impaled on his stick. He brought it to the lantern to give us a better look. Mangled and broken, yet still struggling to get free, it remained the size of a tennis ball.

Holy shit. I'm glad I'll be spending the night in my Bus.

"Araña del plátano. Ellas vienen desde Brasil. Matan a mucha gente."

Moose looked a little worried. "He says it's a banana spider. I heard about 'em the last time I was here. Some baby ones hitched a ride on a boat from Ecuador or something. Now they're spreading all through the plantations here. Oh yeah, he also said they've killed a lot of people."

Oh yeah? That's kind of an important thing to know, isn't it? This was completely nuts. I mean the guy squashed a big-ass scorpion with his sandal like it was commonplace, and made quick work of a nest-full of pissed off hornets. No problema. Then he finds the king of all spiders, and that's *the thing that gets his attention?!*

Our friend waved his hand, palm up, around the shed, as a maître d' would address the most desirable table in the finest of restaurants:

"Es seguro aquí ahora. Duerman bien, mis amigos." ("It is safe here now. Sleep well, my friends.")

His work completed, the fisherman drove off, leaving us to his shed for the night.

"Okay you guys. Get whatever you want out of my Bus. I'll be staying out there tonight, windows closed and doors locked!"

I'll give them credit. Both laid out bedrolls on the dirt floor and made like they were going to spend the night in there. The storm grew louder and more intense. Simultaneous lightning and thunder claps were going off every minute or two. Fierce downpours of rain—the deluge creating such a racket on the tin shed—it roared *inside* the 1DRBUS.

Twenty minutes in, Jelly was first to crack. He tapped on my window and sheepishly asked if he could sleep on the floor under the end of my bed. He said the lantern ran out of fuel, and he was worried about one of those spiders sneaking up on him in the dark. Moose slinked in about a half hour afterward and tried to fashion a bed across the front two seats. Me? I was comfortably stretched out in my snug-without-bugs, full-size bed. Flash … *KABOOM!* This, *suckers!*

The storm blew through by morning, but we waited until midday for things to dry out before attempting the drive back to La Ticla. We never did see our fisherman friend again before we left town. We figured he was probably out chasing another shark.

Our overnight accommodations in El Faro.

A short run in the jungle

Our camp in La Ticla was exactly as we'd left it with the exception of two soccerball-size holes in the palapa roof. I wondered if more people are killed by that damn banana spider, or by coconuts dropping forty feet onto their heads while they slept? Besides the two in our camp, there were several more of the fallen brown husks scattered on the ground nearby. The storm had without question blown through here pretty hard last night, too.

The best thing—after nearly a week of waiting—there was finally some good surf out front the next morning! Nothing ridiculous, just solid six-foot waves with an occasional set that looked every bit of eight feet. It was the perfect size to get back into the swim of things (pun intended).

Most surfers are partial to riding waves that take them one direction over the other. "Regular foot" is riding left foot forward, facing the wave as you take it to your right. Going the other way (right foot forward) and favoring waves that you can ride to your left is called "goofy foot." No one knows for sure where the terms originated, but they are a permanent fixture in the surfing culture. Moose and Jelly were both regulars, and me a goofy.

La Ticla is a classic point break, a bulge in the coastline formed by countless cycles of muddy storm water pouring into the ocean via the arroyo, the debris settling to the bottom. The preferred wave for me was to the north of the point (where I could go left), and the other two guys stayed to the south. The distance between the two breaks depended upon how big the surf was at any given time. When the swell was small it would roll in, break as a single peak, and two of us might take off on the same wave, each riding in the opposite direction of the other: "Split peas" in the ever-evolving surfer's lexicon.

Larger waves would dictate that we might be fifty yards apart, or more, happily doing our own thing.

Our first real session since arriving, we stayed out all morning. Taking a break only to paddle in, eat something, and guzzle some water. It was the most fun I'd ever had surfing, and I wore the grin to show it. The afternoon paddle out was into waves that were getting bigger, consistently exceeding ten feet in size. (The "face" of a wave, the part of it that you see from shore, could be eighteen to twenty feet high on a ten-foot wave. Trust me, it's big.). This made it necessary to increase the distance between me and the other guys until we were always at least 100 to 150 yards apart. Getting closer than that to the peak of a large breaking wave at La Ticla might get you caught "inside." That's what it's called when the waves are breaking farther out than you are, and you find yourself mired in a slog of turbulent white water, unable to easily paddle much of anywhere.

The other way to get caught inside was to screw up on the wave you were riding and get lunched by it. Not "launched." That's what the lip of the wave does as it breaks. I mean, "lunched." "Stuck in the laundry." "Parked in the tow-away zone." All of them, interchangeable terms for finding yourself on the wrong side of a set of large, angry waves. At its worst, its grip can leave you violently tumbling head over heels in the soup, unsure of where top and bottom are. Adding injury to insult—once you figure out where up is—the sudsy froth doesn't offer enough resistance to pull a decent swim stroke against. It can hold you in a state of suspended animation until you eventually reach the surface. It's never fun, especially when the surf is huge and breaking hard.

Sure enough, on my first ten-foot-plus wave of the afternoon session, I kooked out and found myself in the washing machine, stuck on full rinse. After the initial cycle, I got my bearings long enough to reach the top and gulp some air before the thick lip of the next wave crashed on me. It took me deep, bouncing me hard off the sandy bottom. My board was pulled away so violently the leash tethering me to it snapped like an old rubber band. Now it was just me and the suds. There would be no board to cling to until I was able to escape the impact zone and retrieve it from the beach.

Each wave of the set grew larger—and broke more forcefully—than the one before it. Over and over, I battled to reach the top for a single, quick gasp of air before being callously shoved to the bottom again. By the fifth or sixth round, I wondered how much longer I could sustain the strength and steady nerves necessary to find the surface, one more time.

Finally the last wave of the huge set passed, granting me a stay. The strong undertow had carried me along the shore far enough I now found myself in a patch of calm water at the northern fringe of the break. I was coughing, spitting, and sucking in air like a newborn in the delivery room. Well-defined ringlets, on the otherwise glassy surface of the water, radiated from my chest. The dominant ones in perfect tempo with my coughing, the rest in sync with the pounding of my heart. I was in a fog, not completely confident of which was the best direction to swim. Do I head farther outside, and then north until I'm clear of the impact zone? Or straight in, and hope the next big set doesn't overtake me before I get inside far enough?

I looked south, toward where Moose and Jelly were surfing. I thought it might help me figure out which direction to swim if I knew where they were in relation to me—and part of me wanted to see if they'd even noticed how close I'd come to drowning. Sitting atop their boards, Jelly looked frantic, arms waving overhead, and Moose was yelling something, both hands cupped to his face. My ears full of water, I could barely make it out … but it sounded … a little like, …

"SHARK!"

Come on you guys. Seriously. That's not even a little funny.

I waved back, closed my eyes, and kept treading water, working to steady my breathing and regain my senses.

"Opterrrrrs! Goddammit Opters! SHARgghk!" Jelly was yelling now too, straining so hard his voice cracked. He sounded frantic, so I opened my eyes and looked in their direction again. They were both pointing and gesturing wildly for me to look offshore from where I was.

This had better not be a joke. Actually, maybe that would be better …

There it was. A shark fin cleaving the surface of the water. Less than fifty yards away and closing, tacking a line about forty-five degrees from right to left. It was at least as large as the one we had helped the fishermen with in El Faro the day before yesterday.

I never did get the answer to whether it was the kind that ate people …

I watched as it slipped under the water.

Remain calm. They sense panic. Okay, … then what?

There it was again—half the distance this time—tacking left to right, lazily zigzagging ever closer.

If you're trying to scare the shit out of me, it's working! No, mustn't panic.

I treaded water as smoothly as I could.

Maybe it's just cruising around and hasn't sensed me yet? Yeah, right.

I managed to slow my breathing, but my heart was racing so hard and so fast, the ripples in the water departed my chest like grooves on a vinyl record album. The shark dipped below the surface one more time. Its next tack would have it directly on course to me when (or if) it showed itself again.

More than a little preoccupied with the shark, I didn't notice the first wave of another big set rolling in, until I felt its pull, cresting between me and the path of the shark. The closest thing I can compare the next few seconds to was me as a cartoon flying fish. In sheer panic—my arms and legs a blur—I swam into the wave and somehow managed to stay in the white water, pushed along with it, all the way to the shallows. Absolutely convinced I was going to be savagely devoured at any second, I high-stepped it from the ocean and onto the beach like I was barefoot on a bed of hot coals. Rendered completely irrationally unaware by fear, I didn't stop running until both of my feet were bloodied by cobblestones and scrub plants, fifty or sixty yards deep into the jungle.

CHAPTER 9

MAKING A BREAK FOR IT

The beaches of Normandy

The swell lasted for almost a week, but Moose and Jelly were the only ones to enjoy it. As much an excuse as it was my reality, I reasoned the fresh cuts and scrapes on my feet and ankles were surely enough to attract another shark, and I wanted no part of that. I shot several hours of film of the guys ripping on a bunch of really good waves. My new Nikon XL8S Super-8 camera did everything as advertised and more. Telephoto lens with power zoom. Slow motion and freeze frame. Fade in, fade out. It was incredible. Given time, I thought I might get over it. But every time a roll was finished, labeled, and put away, I felt worse. It would never be possible to watch any of this without being tortured by guilt over what I'd done to the previous owner's film. All joy had been sucked from it.

We'd already picked through the mounds of driftwood closest to the river mouth, so each new day meant we had to venture farther north along the shoreline to find pieces dried enough to burn. The guys had let me skip my turn to collect wood for a few days because of my feet, but by day four they'd had enough of me skating, and I couldn't get out of it again. I wasn't the least bit stoked to be the one assigned to firewood duty that particular afternoon. Foreshadowing a repeat performance of what we'd gone through in El Faro the week before, the sky had been darkening since midday. We could hear the occasional soft rumble of distant thunder from somewhere out over the ocean. It was now or never, so I walked a few hundred yards up the beach at dusk and began gathering wood.

The first visible lightning flashed down the beach to the south a ways and I counted, "one–one thousand, two–one thousand, three–one thousand, four–one thousand, five–crack-rumble" ... *Almost five miles away. No worries.*

Flash! That one seemed a lot closer. Sure enough, my count was interrupted by a loud *KABOOM!* before I finished, "two–one thous ..." *Fuck this. With what I'm carrying, we have plenty of wood for tonight. I'm done.* Flash–*KABOOM! Holy shit!* A bolt actually hit the middle of a coconut palm grove just off the beach a few decent stone throws south of our palapa. The flash was blinding, the shockwave rippled my flesh.

Jogging now, one of the pieces I was carrying jostled free and fell at my feet, so I paused and turned to retrieve it. Flash–*KABOOM–BOOM!* A bolt struck the jungle in front of me and another went off simultaneously on the beach to my rear. I swear I felt the tingle of electricity in the sand under my feet, and the air suddenly had a strange *pool-chemical* odor to it. Spectacular spider webs of arc-welder-intense light were everywhere, reaching sea, sand, and jungle on three sides of me now. My ears rang from the unyielding cacophony.

Fuck that. I dropped the rest of the wood I was carrying and launched into a dead run across the beach toward the palapa.

What is this? Fucking Normandy?! When do the machine guns open up on me?

"Didn't know if you were going to make it! Where's the wood?"

"Yeah, Opters. Ack-ack-ack-ack. Where's the firewood?"

I didn't have time to catch my breath and spit out an answer before a blast of wind and ridiculous torrent of rain prompted all three of us to take cover in the 1DRBUS. Flash … *KABOOM!* thundered directly overhead, followed by the distinctive *ka-whump!* sound of a coconut punching through the roof of our palapa outside.

I still was breathing hard, "Whadaya say … we try … somewhere else … for a few days?"

"Manzanillo. The guy I got the pot from said he heard there are three American surfer chicks in Manzanillo. He said a big storm might be coming near here in a couple of days, too."

So, this *isn't a big storm?*

"How big a storm?"

"He said the crews are moving all their construction equipment to the other side of the river for a couple of days, just in case it gets bad here."

When were you going to share this little tidbit, Moose? Fuck it. I don't care. I just want to get the hell out of here.

"Let's pack up and leave after breakfast tomorrow, okay?"
Shit, I'd leave now if we weren't under attack!

"That depends on how the surf is in the morning. If it's firing like it was yesterday, we're staying here. Who knows when I'll have this chance again?" Moose, making his priorities clear.

Jelly chipped in. "Much more rain and the river may keep us here, anyway."

Now, that'd suck.

As luck would have it, the surf was perfect the next morning, so the guys went out. Hoping for the best, I stayed in camp and started packing up to leave. A feeling of profound emptiness washed over me. Here I was in La Ticla, having finally surfed one of the coveted jewels of mainland Mexico. Once. That was it. One morning for about five hours. And now I was alone in camp, stowing our stuff so we could leave. I sat there staring at nothing in particular, spellbound by the moment. It was sobering to think of how much of me I had squandered, in vain pursuit of being accepted, instead of putting that same energy into living a life that was worth something.

Mr. Recker's cooler

I'm not sure how late it was when the guys returned to camp, but it was well after lunch. I was glad to see them, because the skies were beginning to get ugly again. Of course, Moose had to eat and smoke some pot before we could get going. Nonetheless, we broke camp half an hour later.

We motored slowly up the muddy main drag through the village until we reached the La Ticla–El Faro road, turned left, and made our way back to the arroyo. Reminiscent of the day we'd first arrived, two large dump trucks were readying to cross, a group of peasants gathered off to one side, hoping to hitch a ride north. The water bore a curious burnt-red hue, and appeared it might be moving a tad faster than before. Possibly a bit wider, too, but I didn't think it looked any deeper. It was still just a broad, muddy wash with a dirt trail dipping in on one side and reappearing on the other. We got out and watched each driver ahead of us wave aboard a load of men, women, and children before fording the stream. The trucks had brief moments where they bogged down and nearly got stuck, but each made it successfully, just as they had the other day.

The last truck safely on the other side, it was our turn to go. An old and palpably road-weary couple walked slowly over to us, hunched over and saddled with homemade cloth packs (nearly as tall as they were) bound tightly with coarse twine. They didn't need to say anything; their deeply creased, weather-beaten faces and sun-reddened eyes told all that was necessary. They wanted us to ferry them across.

"Hey Opters. These people want our help getting across."
No shit Moose.

"I don't see what good that'll do us. We're already topped out on weight as it is. I don't wanna risk getting bogged down in the mud. Tell them we're sorry, but, No." *Boy that sounded heartless. Whatever. I just want to get the fuck out of here.*

"Really, Opters? That's not cool. But, it's your call."

"Yes, really. C'mon man. It's our turn. Tell 'em, so we can go." I was starting to get a little freaked out by this whole thing. The skies to the east were ominous shades of gray, and the river was getting uglier by the minute.

Moose pulled his door closed and stuck his face out the window. "Mi amigo es un gilipollas. Él dice qué no tenemos espacio para ti." ("My friend is an asshole. He says we don't have room for you.")

The old couple didn't say anything in return. The man cast his eyes downward and shook his head resignedly. The woman convicted me with a piercing glare. Her eyes told not of disappointment over refusing them, but of a silent fury for disrespecting her husband in front of her.

I sent a villager on ahead with my camera to capture my triumph on film, cocksure we'd make it across the river.

Rolling into the wash, I was doing my best to think positively, because we'd done this before. All that changed about halfway across. The ruts between the rocks were deeper and more pronounced. The current was markedly faster and more powerful, forcing us to "crab" into it to maintain our heading. The rear wheels lost their traction for a second, and our back end pivoted a few feet downstream. The force of the water bounced us ass-end first into an eddy deep enough that the engine gurgled and coughed, having been submerged to the carburetor ever so briefly.

"Holy shit! Is this pig going to make it or what?"

"Stop calling it a goddamned pig, Moose! ... I don't know."

I steered more upstream to escape the eddy and make it back onto the same path the dump trucks had followed. The current was relentlessly bullying us now, pushing us around. I pressed the accelerator pedal to the floor to overcome the twin foes of fast water and the low spot we'd been backed into. The front of the Bus pitched up, lifted by the water rushing under it, just as the deep tread of the rear tires tore into the bottom. The 1DRBUS reared like a stallion and mounted itself squarely atop a submerged boulder. We were high-centered in such a way that none of our four tires touched solid ground any longer. I gunned the engine and turned the front wheels side to side without any real effect, except for pivoting us back to perpendicular with the river again. We were stuck bigger than shit.

"Now what do we do, Opters?"

"We have to get off this goddamned rock! Both of you get out and see if you can push us forward."

The current was getting stronger by the minute. It obviously was raining hard upstream, and we had to get to one side or the other. *Now!* Between the bad footing and surging water, the guys didn't have any luck pushing us forward off the rock, so we had to come up with another plan.

"Both of you stand on the back bumper and see if you can get the rear wheels to make contact with the bottom. I'll put it in reverse and maybe we can *back* off of here!"

Following him in the passenger-side mirror, I watched Moose deliberately make his way along the upstream side of the Bus, plainly wary of losing his footing. At the rear, he looked back at me and shook his head. I didn't warn him in time not to use the custom air scoop as a handhold, and watched as he ripped it free from the side of the Bus.

This is painful. I'm watching everything I treasure, being destroyed in front of my eyes.

It was pointless. There was no amount of moving or rocking the Bus enough, for any of its four tires to so much as graze the bottom.

Making my way to the back to join Moose and Jelly, I spotted the old couple on the shore, a dozen men grouped behind them. I cupped both hands to my face and yelled as loud as I could to be heard over the din of the water.

"Hey!!! Hey!!! Can you help us, por favor?! POR FAVOR!"

"Moose! Ask them to help us! Please, ask 'em! Why the fuck are they all just standing there watching?"

I yelled again, "Por favor, amigos!"

"They're not going to help us. You insulted 'em. They'd rather watch us drown."

Oh my God! Please!

"Please Moose! Please! Just ask 'em! How do I tell them I'm sorry?"

"Lo siento, but it's not gonna help. They're a proud people. You caused them to lose face, and now we're fucked. *You* did this."

"¡Lo Siento! Lo Siento! Por favor! GODDAMMIT YOU FUCKERS! LO SIENTO!"

And with that, first the old couple, and then the others, turned their backs on us and walked away.

"We're done, Opters. Your Bus isn't going anywhere. I'm grabbing my board and the rest of my shit and headin' back to the palapa."

Jelly looked at me helplessly for a second. His expression said it all before he opened his mouth. "I'm with Moose. We aren't getting outta here tonight. Let's get whatever we can to dry ground. We can try again in the morning."

Moose was inside, roughly pulling things from under the bed, separating his belongings (including the last dozen or so of his dirty magazines) from the rest of our gear, and leaving anything that wasn't his, strewn across the floor. He collected everything he'd brought except for his board, and made his way back to the Ticla side of the river. The water, unrelenting in its rise, threatened to push the Bus off the rock and onto its side.

"Jelly! We need to close the barn doors and open both front doors so the water can flow through, and not tip us over!"

He'd already grabbed as much as he could carry and yelled, "I'll be right back!"

God, I hope so. I've no chance of winning this battle on my own.

I managed to get the barn doors closed and the front ones opened on my own. The water poured into the passenger door faster than it could empty out the driver's side and surged up and over the walk-through between the front seats, inundating the galvanized steel box that I'd welded to the floor last year. (The very same "lockbox" that made my killer stereo, twin amplifiers, and all my tapes near impossible to snatch.) Nothing I could do about it now. The water was overtopping the box and spilling into the back of the Bus where all our gear was stowed. I grabbed whatever was on the floor, or still under the bed, and began tossing it up onto the mattress to keep it from getting any wetter. Outside, Moose was back and spewing profanities, working to free his surfboard from the roof racks. Jelly, having completed a trip to the riverbank and wading toward the Bus, yelled for Moose to grab his board, too. He ignored him and started back to shore with only *his* board under one arm, the mesh bag holding his fins, mask, and snorkel cradled in the other. As they met halfway, I could only imagine the conversation between the supposed friends. The water continued to rise, and Jelly struggled to make it back to the Bus without being knocked off his feet and swept downstream.

"Fuck him, the selfish prick!" were the first words I could make out over the roar of the water. "Let's just put our boards inside the Bus and carry whatever else we can back to shore!"

Either Jelly is becoming more human, or less like Moose ... I suppose that's one and the same.

"Okay. Can you take care of the boards? I need to get my cameras out of here! Everything worth saving is on the bed."

Rather than try to climb through from the front again, I maneuvered to the back of the Bus and lifted the hatch. The water hadn't yet reached the level of the bed, and the crate with my cameras still was dry. As carefully as possible, I rested the crate on top of the Bus and held open the hatch for Jelly. He retrieved a box of his own things, handed it to me, and then stashed our boards inside before slamming the rear hatch closed. It was too much to try and carry more than one thing at a time amid the fight to remain upright in the rushing water. We weren't sure if we'd be able to make another trek back to the Bus, so we each grabbed what was most important to us and made our way to the riverbank. Though it was only late afternoon, the sky was nearly black, the storm clouds that'd lurked inland were sliding toward us—and it began to rain.

"I think we should make another trip to the Bus." I pleaded. "Our stove, food, drinking water, and most of our clothes are still out there."

"Not to mention our boards, Opters."

"C'mon Moose. Quit being so goddamned selfish and help us get the rest of it."

I guess Jelly has finally had his fill of Moose.

"Nah, you guys go ahead. I'm gonna stay here and keep an eye on my stuff."

Unbelievable.

"So be it. We have to go now or forget it. C'mon, Opters."

Wow. Every bit as unbelievable. Who are these guys, and what have they done with Moose and Jelly?

Paul Wilson

It's getting dark, my Bus is perched atop a submerged boulder in the middle of the Ostula River, and the water is rising fast. Moose's top priority is saving his bedroll and his little box of pot.

The river was barely passable. The increasing current and lousy footing dropped each of us on our asses a few times. It took everything we had in us to reach the Bus. Several feet short, a growing rumble, mimicking the sound white water makes when a big wave breaks, caused us to pause. It was coming from upstream and just visible through the raindrops. A roiling, three-foot-high mound of water was charging at us, riding atop the already chest-deep current and rounding the bend up canyon. It was a nasty, out-of-control caldron of dirty brown froth, uprooted bushes, pieces of trees, and what appeared to be most of a hut. Ghostly surreal in the dim light, it took a few moments to understand what it was.

"Flash flood!!! Flash flood!!!"

It was apparent we had only fifteen or twenty seconds to react. Jelly looked at me wild-eyed. "Swim for it!!!"

Before he could gather himself to go, a blood-curdling wail pierced the white-noise roar of the approaching maelstrom. A young calf (or maybe it was a goat), captured in a snarl of broken branches, was helplessly somersaulting before the unholy mess, desperately shrieking for mama. It was beyond calamitous, and every base instinct pushed me to join Jelly in panic, but a paralyzing fear of drowning wouldn't allow me.

"It's too late! That tangle of shit'll take us under, too! We have to stay here!"

I was already on the roof when Jelly reached me. "C'mon! Let's try to keep the Bus between us and all that crap! Grab a board rack and don't let go, no matter what!"

Each of us could only get a "life or death" type of grip on one rack at a time. I wrapped my left arm around the front one, Jelly hugged the rear rack with his right, and we locked our free arms between us. Caught somewhere between ready and terror, we hung off the downstream side of the roof and awaited the inevitable.

"Here goes nothing!"

"God help us!" I pleaded in return.

Looking past Jelly, I saw Moose pitch his board up into the jungle, it being the only thing to escape the initial rout of water and debris that tore up the bank and swallowed him, *and* all of the things we'd moved to higher ground. Jelly didn't see it happen; his focus was on timing our own impact, taking deep breaths in preparation for holding it as long as possible. The torrent launched up and over, before punching down hard enough to knock the wind out of us. The 1DRBUS lifted and heaved onto its side, finally dislodging from its perch atop that damned boulder. Jelly and I were dragged underwater, but spared major impact or entanglement by the larger debris that dominated the leading edge of the deluge.

Spun around by the debris-laden water, the Bus righted itself as the weight of its engine pulled the back end under again. Somehow, the front remained above water, and the treacherous initial wave of the flash flood filled in around us. The swift current pinned both front doors open wide like the ears on Dumbo the Flying Elephant. Sporting these oversize water wings like sails, we were dragged relentlessly downstream toward the ocean. We caught sight of Moose up ahead of us, bear-hugging Mr. Recker's red-and-white Coleman cooler. He was circling the middle of an angry eddy that churned and spun between us and the riverbank. I considered calling out to him, but Jelly and I were preoccupied with fending off all manner of floating muck and rubble, pummeling us about our heads and shoulders.

The arroyo widened as it neared the coast, and blessedly the water spread out, slowed, and got shallower. We'd ridden atop the 1DRBUS for over a mile before it snagged on the bottom and came to a stop. The rain had eased off, and it felt like the worst of the flood had passed. In the dim twilight, the whites of our eyes and our teeth contrasted sharply with the burnt-red mud that coated everything else.

"Well that sucked." Jelly said, through a sputtering cough.

Truer words were never spoken.

"Are you hurt?" It was the first thing I could think of to ask Jelly—not exactly sure about myself …

"No, I'm okay, but it looks like we may be spending the night out h..."

Different from the sounds made by the other crap hitting and scraping along the Bus, a hollow sounding *thunk-screeee* interrupted Jelly. It was Mr. Recker's red-and-white Coleman cooler—and no Moose in sight.

"Moose! Are you out there? Moose!" Jelly's voice was hoarse and not much more than a loud whisper, his throat raw from choking on dirty water. He teared up, undoubtedly worried, frustrated, and in pain.

"He probably got out and just left the cooler to float away, Jelly. You know how he's been."

"Yeah, you're probably right. I can't yell anymore."

We spent the night on top of the Bus, too exhausted to do anything else. At first light, we saw the water level had dropped; it looked to be no more than waist-deep at most. Jelly eased himself off the roof and rested his foot atop the front, passenger-side tire, fully intending to hop down from there and make his way to shore. Overnight, the persistent rush of water around the Bus had eroded the sandy bottom like a receding wave does to a stone on the beach. He discovered too late that a deep moat now surrounded us, and the water topped his shoulders before he got his feet under him.

"Fucking shit, Opters! We're perched on a goddamned hill again!"

"Hola!" One of the villagers emerged from the jungle growth carrying a coil of rope and waded into the water.

"Hola! Buenos dias!" *Well, maybe not so bueno, but I'm happy as hell to see him!*

When near enough, he tossed the rope to us, and Jelly wrapped a couple of turns around the roof rack before tying it off. The villager retreated to the Ticla side of the wash and lashed his end of the lifeline around a coconut palm trunk. Jelly was first to reach dry land with me right on his heels, though I'd left a shoe buried deep—sucked from my foot by the sticky red mud along the way.

"Gracias! Gracias mucho!" My Spanish probably wasn't correct, and I fought the urge to pick him up and swing him around like he'd just told me this had all been a bad dream.

"De nada, de nada." He looked to be only about twenty-five or thirty years old, but his yellowed and blackened teeth made him appear much older.

Neither of us knew for sure what he was saying, so we took turns shaking his hand, all the while repeating, "Gracias! Gracias!"

Pointing toward the beach, he said something much too quickly for either of us to have a clue what it is: "Tu amigo está recogiendo tus cosas en la playa." ("Your friend is collecting your stuff from the beach.")

"¿Qué? Más despacio, por favor." ("What? Slow down, please.")

Wow. Jelly knows a bit of Spanish after all.

"Tu amigo está recogiendo tus cosas en la playa." Every bit as fast and unintelligible as before.

I gave it a try. "No comprende mi amigo." *Hope that's close.* ("My friend does not understand.")

Our new friend tilted his head in puzzlement, faced Jelly, and pared it to a minimum for us: "Ustedes son amigos. ¿Sí?" pointing at each of us in turn.

"Sí. Sí. We are amigos." Jelly, with an accompanying thumbs up.

Okay. That's been established.

Enunciating every syllable: "Tu o-tro a-mi-go es-ta en la play-a," he said while he swept his outstretched arm toward the beach.

"Moose is on the beach!" Jelly reacting as a lottery winner. "He's telling us Moose is on the beach!"

Dead or alive?

"Sí! Sí! En la playa!"

"Gracias amigo! Gracias a lot!"

"De nada, de nada!"

We thanked our new friend again and peeled off toward the beach in search of Moose. The sandbar that had previously restrained the river was gone, pushed well into the surf zone. Even so, it was possible to hopscotch over to the north bank, jumping from hump to hump of marooned driftwood and debris.

Moose was waiting for us on the other side, a pile of wet belongings at his feet,

"Hey, you made it! I wasn't too sure."

"Yeah Moose. We can see how worried you were, out here picking through our crap on the beach and all …" *I wasn't at all convinced he gave a whit.*

Jelly acted like everything was forgiven. "What happened to you? We saw you with Mr. Recker's cooler, and then it floated by without you later. I thought maybe you drowned or something."

"Yeah, were you wondering if maybe *we'd* drowned, Moose?"

"Nah, I saw you on that pig of a Bus when you rolled by. Thanks for seeing if I was okay and everything," Moose fired back snarkily.

Oh well …

"No big deal. I caught onto a bush and pulled myself out."

"And Mr. Recker's cooler?" I asked, already knowing the answer.

"I was done with it, let it go." Bingo! There's the Moose we know. "Don't get your panties in a wad, though. It's over there on the beach with some of your crap."

"What else have you found? Most my clothes are gone, and my cash was in a pants pocket." *Whoops. I shouldn't have let on that my money was out there somewhere.*

"Yeah, I found your Levi's in the bushes by the river mouth. No money in 'em, though."

Right. My last sixty-five dollars was in those pants, you fucker.
"There was a five-dollar bill on the beach, though."

I reached my hand toward Moose. "Well, if that's *all* you really found, I'll take it and go look for the rest."

"No one knows if it's your five-dollar bill. It wasn't with anyone's stuff. I found it. It's mine now."

"You're kidding, right?"

"C'mon, Moose!" Jelly mustered a raspy yell. "Give the guy his money already! Fuck! He's already lost everything else!"

"Look. I didn't tell him to drive into the goddamned river! He did that on his own. And if he'd just given those people a ride, the whole fucking town would have carried that worthless pig of a Volkswagen to the other side on their fucking shoulders!"

Moose turned his wrath on me directly, jabbing a stubby finger into my chest. "Opters, you're fucking lucky I found most of my stuff, or you'd owe me for that, too. Fuck you and your five dollars. It's mine now."

"Fuck you, Moose. Get your own ride home." *Not quite as impactful as that would be if the 1DRBUS wasn't in the middle of the Ostula-fucking-river!*

Moose gathered up his stuff and walked somewhat stiff legged, off toward the palapa where he'd already reestablished himself. Jelly and I spent the next couple of hours canvassing the beach and river mouth for our gear. Satisfied we'd found all that was findable on the beach, Jelly said we should take it back to the palapa. We agreed: He'll handle that chore, and I'll head back upstream along the riverbank, in hopes of retrieving more of our things still ensnared by the mud.

I continued my search all the way upstream to the spot where we'd tried to rescue our crates and boxes to high ground at the crossing. The old couple was there and saw me coming. The woman beckoned me over. I was expecting to be dealt a load of grief. Instead, there, laid out in front of her on a little old blanket, was my movie camera and a dozen waterlogged boxes of film. I was in shock, embarrassed and ashamed by my behavior the afternoon before. My shoulders slumped forward, my chin dropped slowly, and I mumbled softly,

"Lo siento."

The old woman deferred to her husband, who responded with a quiet, "De nada."

Wow, "No worries," after the shameful way I treated them ...? I need to thank them in a way that'll mean something ... and maybe help to assuage my guilt a little?

"Yo no tiene dinero for you." I stumbled through trying to let them know I didn't have any money to offer them as a reward.

The woman looked directly into my eyes and shook her head ever so slightly. She raised her tiny hand, palm facing me, work-worn, crooked fingers in the air: "Alto. De nada."

It burned into me, etched across my heart: *"Stop. No worries." No grudge. No greed. No worries?*

A pig in a poke

The old woman insisted I keep her small blanket and tied it into a neat bundle, with my camera and rolls of exposed film inside for the walk back to the palapa. The guys already had a fire going and were making coffee. Moose had recovered it, his baggie of pot, and bottle of mezcal from the beach.

"Hey. Can I get some coffee, or is that yours now, too?" *Who knows what new rules Moose will come up with ...*

He fired back, "Do you want the rest of your clothes or not? I found the bag with your mom's camera, some papers, and car registration, too. It all looks okay."

I'll keep quiet for now and take what I can get.

"Miguel, my friend from the construction crew … you know … the guy with the pot, said he can get a dump truck and pull your pig out of the river for twenty dollars."

Ignoring the "pig" dig, I answered back, "Yeah, well I don't have twenty dollars to give him anymore. Maybe you have it?"

"Look, Opters, I didn't take your fucking money! I have my own cash, and I'm not about to pay for your mistakes."

Yeah. Like I thought you'd volunteer … "Whatever. Let's see if he'll take something in trade. Maybe he'd like this fancy movie camera that's been underwater all night?"

Jelly jumped in. "Wow! You found it? Where?"

"Not me. The old couple found it. They were waiting at the crossing when I got there."

"You're learning about the *real* Mexicans, Opters. They'd rather keep their honor than steal your shit."

Says the guy with no honor, and holding my cash.

"My friend is gonna come back with his truck. You can ask him if he wants any of your shit then."

Miguel and his dump truck rumbled up to the palapa about an hour later. I ended up trading him my diving watch for his help. He backed into the river as far as he dared to. Jelly and I waded out to the Bus, where we wrapped and bolted the free end of Miguel's heavy chain to the top of the spare-tire mount. Miguel gunned his engine and the big truck rumbled forward a few feet. The chain snapped to attention, drawing tight enough to tightrope walk across. The only part of the 1DRBUS that moved was the spare-tire mount, twisting down and to one side, the torque mangling the left front panel below the windshield.

Paul Wilson

His truck already chained to my Bus, Miguel used the hydraulics of his dump bed to try and free the rear wheels, buried deep in the mud. (Note the "high-water" mark on the opposite riverbank, behind the truck. At peak flood, only the Bus's rooftop surfboard racks were visible.)

He tried twice again to yank the Bus free, before climbing from his truck, unfastening his end of the chain, and dropping it into the water. I figured he was going to try and get closer or lined up more directly in front of us. Instead, he climbed up into his truck's cab and tried to move it, first forward and then in reverse, with nothing but water spun from his rear tires to show for it. His truck was stuck fast in the river, right along with the 1DRBUS. Not going anywhere soon, all three of us waded back to shore. Miguel wasted no time in walking off toward the bridge construction crew, and soon returned riding shotgun in another dump truck, the bed of this one carrying a complement of twelve to fifteen villagers.

The driver approached us, grinned, and pointed to his wrist. He was wearing the watch that I'd traded to Miguel for pulling us out.

Fine with me. Just get my Bus out of the goddamned river!

Miguel said he still needed to get paid for his troubles, too, so we worked it out. If my Bus was delivered to a small clearing about one hundred feet from the river bank, I'd give him my camp stove, too.

The second truck was soon backed into the river, halfway out to Miguel's truck, where the two trucks and the 1DRBUS were "daisy-chained" (pun intended) together. Once the three of us were linked, fifteen to twenty minutes of yanking and maneuvering—accompanied by a steady stream of chatter, groans, and applause from the villagers—elapsed before my Bus was finally dragged into the clearing. The interior still held at least a foot of water, with another foot of mud layered under that. It took a few minutes to locate and extricate the promised stove from the mud, but Miguel was happy to receive it. With a "Vaya con Dios!" from both drivers, they, and the audience of curious villagers, left us alone with our mess.

It required two full-size dump trucks linked together
to finally free my Bus from the sticky mud.

167

Jelly and I set up a makeshift camp in the clearing. Moose stayed at the palapa by the beach during the days (I suspect to avoid being asked to help), but after the first night, joined our little camp each evening (probably because that's where the food was). After we'd removed a few hundred pounds of mud and cleaned the things we could salvage, I set about seeing if I could somehow get the engine going again. Pulling the dipstick for the oil told me pretty much all I needed to know, when a pencil-thick stream of dirty water jetted up out of the hole. I put the dipstick back in and removed it again to check the level. No oil. Only water. I guess when an engine is underwater long enough, the oil rises to the surface of the water the engine is under? Whatever, it was going to require a full teardown and rebuild to ever run again.

A few of the several hundred pounds of "Ostula Fudge"
that had settled inside overnight.

Somewhat ironically, the storm that'd spooked us into making a break for it (precipitating our doomed flight from Paradise) never developed beyond the up-canyon deluge that punched our ticket on the abortive river crossing.

While I waited for the others to get back from surfing, I worked out my plan. First, pack everything I still owned, back into my Bus (since I couldn't count on the guys to take care of, or keep an eye on *any* of it). Next, hitch a ride into Tecomán and call my mom to see if she could help bail me out of this mess by sending me some money. Then, hire someone to tow the 1DRBUS back across the river—which had receded to a mere trickle—and take it to a place in Tecomán that could rebuild the engine.

When the guys returned, I explained what was up with the engine and laid out my plan. They were just as happy to stay in La Ticla, surf some more, and let me do the legwork anyway, so we all agreed that's what would happen. I asked Moose for the five dollars again, so I could at least have *some* cash on me for my trip to Tecomán. At first he refused, but then grudgingly agreed to "loan" it to me as long as I promised to repay him when I got back.

Fucking Moose.

I'd already packed what I needed so I could leave first thing in the morning.

We built a fire and cooked some fish that Moose got from a villager. After dinner, he broke out what was left in his bottle of mezcal. "Hey, let's celebrate and finish this off."

"Celebrate what?"

Yeah, Jelly. I'd like to know, too.

"Lots of things, man! Celebrate that our boards didn't get trashed in the flood. Celebrate that I found my weed and my bottle of mezcal. Celebrate that I found five dollars to lend to Opters for his trip to Tecomán. ... See, there's lots to celebrate!"

You've got to be kidding.

"You guys go ahead. I don't want to have a headache all the way to Tecomán."

"Ah, c'mon Opters! Ack-ack-ack-ack ... It'll be fine!"

You mean "gack-gack-gack-gack," don't you Jelly?

"You guys each down a shot, and if any's left, I'll do one too." Looking at the bottle, there won't be much if anything for me to worry about.

Using an empty 35mm film container as a shot glass, each downed a full one, leaving me with a half shot. Moose broke out his weed and rolled up a fat joint. By the time we'd burned it, the mezcal was beginning to take effect and we all had a happy buzz on.

Moose started going on about how drugs help him get "religious."

"You mean like, wholly fucked up, Moose?" I quipped, chuckling at my own pun.

"Yeah, like that. All fucked up, and thinkin' about everything. You know, like surfing and eating and sleeping and stuff. You know, like doing those things in different places, and not being in jail or around my dad and stuff."

"Wow. That's some pretty deep thinkin' alright. So when you're getting religious ... I mean ... Moose, in your religion, do you pray for surf and food and staying out of jail, or is there other stuff too?" *Now, I'm just being a smart-ass.*

"Fuck you, Opters. Hey! You hear that over there in those bushes? Shhh ... be quiet a second and listen."

This should be good.

In our "enlightened" condition, staying completely silent for more than a few seconds was a challenge. But sure enough, the sound of dry leaves being crushed underfoot and bushes rustling could be heard over the crackling of our fire. It was impossible to make out anything in the pitch-black of the jungle, especially with the light of our campfire blinding us to it.

In a low whisper, Jelly asked worriedly, "Is ... is there someone sneaking up on us, Moose? Banditos, maybe? What should we do?"

I agreed with Jelly. It was unnerving to hear the crunching of feet creeping around in the jungle close by. Whatever it was, it was successfully staying hidden from us. "Should we put the fire out so we can see better? Maybe yell to 'em so they know we know they're there?"

This was really getting creepy. Like someone was going to burst out of the jungle at any moment and viciously attack us with machetes.

"Awe c'mon, you fucking snivelers. Relax. It ain't nut'n." With that, Moose reached to the ground at his side, and, in a single motion, picked up a tennis-ball-size rock and whipped it high and hard in the general direction of the noise. It nicked a coconut palm trunk before disappearing into the darkness. Another *clack-clunk* as it caromed off a couple more trees ... and then, an unmistakably hollow *thud!* as the stone struck something solid, but fleshy.

"WHEET!-WHEET!-WHEET!-WHEET!-WHEET!" The sudden pandemonium of trampled bushes and breaking limbs shocked our senses. Moose had potshotted a wild pig— in the pitch-black darkness of the jungle—with a rock.

"You see! That's because I got religious! It gives me mystical powers!" Moose saluted us each in turn, seeking (and receiving) congratulatory high fives.

I have to pee. Like right now. Before I wet my pants.

Jelly was laughing so hard he fell off the rock he was sitting on, and darn near stuck his hand in the fire. Tears of laughter flowed from all three of us; my nose had spontaneously begun running. From here on out, I would never question whether Moose "gets religious" when he's high on something.

Sudden impact

For a change, my solo trip into Tecomán the following morning was uneventful. I reached my mom via collect telephone call on the first try. She wired me the three hundred dollars I asked for, and I used part of it on a cheap hotel room for an overdue shower and a good night's rest. Before it got too late in the day, I searched Tecomán in a fruitless quest for the right mechanic. One confident he could successfully rebuild a (still water-filled) VW engine that had been submerged overnight—a week ago.

Everyone I explained the situation to said I should have it towed it to the VW dealership in Colima, located in the mountains, about an hour's drive to the east. One of the garages I visited had a makeshift tow truck that looked like it could do the job. We settled on a price of forty dollars, plus gas, to pick up my Bus in La Ticla and deliver it (and me) to the dealership in Colima.

Before returning to my hotel, I stopped into a small café to have some dinner. There was a dog-eared newspaper on the table where I was seated, and I picked it up, curious to see what qualified as news in Tecomán. Above the fold, in the left-hand column, was an ominous photograph of a jetliner with a wing on fire, and in a steep dive. I was able to make out the gist of the article. A PSA passenger jet had collided with another plane and crashed into a neighborhood back home in San Diego the day before. It said that 137 people were believed to have died on the two planes, and 7 more in the houses on the ground. I wondered why my mom hadn't said anything about it to me when we spoke on the phone earlier. Maybe she thought I had enough to worry about. *I'm ashamed to have whined to her.*

The realization that this tragedy had happened back home—at precisely the same time that I was moping around and feeling sorry for myself on the bank of the Ostula River—threw my run of luck over the last few weeks into an entirely different perspective. Those poor people innocently were going about their lives when disaster struck them down. Good Lord, the people in their houses on the ground never even *knew* they were about to die. I wondered if any of them were like me, guilty of doing a bunch of foolishly dishonest crap. The difference being, they never had an opportunity to seek forgiveness or to make amends. Just, *BLAM!* and they were gone. And here I was being warned repeatedly to get my shit together—or pay an even bigger price than had been extracted already. Fuck me and my pity party. *I* was the fortunate one. My penance may not have been over yet (I didn't doubt for a second there was more hell for me to pay), but I had the opportunity, at least for today, to change the direction I was heading.

El Gran Hotel Colima

Surprisingly, the guys were nearby and ready to leave when my hired tow truck and I crossed the Ostula River and made way down to our impromptu campsite. As funky as the improvised tow truck was, it was evident its owner knew exactly what he was doing. He had the 1DRBUS hooked, secured, and ready to roll out in a few minutes. I rode up front with the driver, Moose and Jelly "wheels up" in the Bus.

After crossing back over that cursed river, we only stopped long enough for gas in Tecomán before continuing up the meandering jungle road to the city of Colima. Much like

Roberto had for us at VW La Paz, the service manager at the VW Colima dealership arranged a place for us to stay. This time, however, instead of a corrugated tin shelter, we were provided a pickup truck's cab-over camper (minus the pickup truck) resting on blocks in an open field on the northern outskirts of Colima.

The camper was an island unto itself. You couldn't even *see* civilization from there. The only thing of note was a huge volcano puffing smoke, way off in the distance. Even so, a teenage boy rode a bicycle out to us with a small basketful of Mexican sweet rolls early the next morning. He asked for one peso (about thirteen cents) each, but we were so grateful for this small kindness, that we bought them all and sent him back with double payment. It shouldn't have been a surprise when he showed up the next day with *two* baskets of pastries and breads in hand!

Paul Wilson

Not found in my AAA travel guide, these were our accommodations in the boonies of Colima.

I waited an extra day before making my way back to the dealership, wanting to give them plenty of time to get everything taken care of. I needn't have done that. The service manager took me in the back and showed me my engine, still in pieces, spread out on a workbench. He did his best to explain: Being submerged so far, and for so long, had displaced all of the oil in the engine in favor of muddy water. The piston rings already had been frozen in place by corrosion, when the mechanic ruined them trying to pry 'em out.

Unfortunately, I had modified my engine by upgrading to oversize cylinders and pistons in an effort to milk a little more power out of it. (After all, it *was* "The Wonderbus." I couldn't very well leave it stock, could I?) He went on to explain, the closest place to Colima selling that type of piston ring was in Mexico City. To make matters worse, because they weren't an authentic VW part, the dealership policy would not permit them to order the rings directly. They insisted the only feasible way for me to get them (especially since I only had cash to pay with) was to take my old rings to the off-road specialty shop in Mexico City—in person—and purchase the new ones myself. Then, and only then, could the VW dealer install the oversize piston rings in my engine. However, none of their work would be guaranteed because of the non-authentic parts used. I argued the situation from every angle, but they wouldn't yield an inch. It was their way or the highway, and well ... you know. ...

Tres Estrellas de Oro (Three Stars of Gold)

Rather than spend another unnecessary night in our Colima camper, I went by the bus station and bought a ticket on the evening bus to Mexico City before going back and giving the guys a heads-up. Tres Estrellas de Oro was the only bus line available out of Colima, and I assumed it was akin to Greyhound as the dominant player on this side of the border. The trip sounded arduous to me, a "red-eye special": Depart Colima at 9 p.m.; a two-hour layover and change of buses in Guadalajara; and then all night to Mexico City, with a scheduled arrival of 9:30 a.m.

Sleep was out of the question on the first leg of the journey, put forth as a three-and-a-half-hour ride from Colima to Guadalajara. Every time I considered laying back and closing my eyes for a minute, our bus would careen through another slalom-curved, white-knuckle, roller-coaster, switchback stretch of mountain road. Neither was there any concern of our driver falling asleep at the wheel. He undeniably embraced the challenge of going absolutely as fast as possible on the narrow highway.

We arrived in Guadalajara at midnight, a full half hour ahead of schedule, and thankfully in one piece. I hadn't brought along anything to eat, and was feeling it. The next leg of the trip was posted as departing for Mexico City in two and a half hours, so, having time on my hands, I stepped outside into the damp, musty-smelling night air and walked completely around the town square in search of an open market or restaurant. Other than a solitary, sketchy-looking taco cart on the corner, I discovered the only place to buy food at this hour was inside the bus station. Even then, the entire selection appeared to be limited to what was available via vending machine. The usual chips, candy, and sodas—plus one display case bearing an assortment of wet, stubby, torpedo-sandwich-looking things wrapped in clear cellophane and secured with Scotch tape.

The candy machine whirred and grinded, failed to deliver anything, but kept my money. Coins inserted into the soda machine rushed feebly to the coin return without any discernable effect. I went to the ticket window and asked for help, relying upon a single semester of middle-school Spanish and hand gestures. The lady behind the bars eventually figured me out, called over the PA system for someone to help, and sent me back over to the row of vending machines to wait. At this hour, I was surprised a bit when it was a preteen kid who skipped over to help me. The half-finished, two-liter bottle of Mountain Dew under his arm explained his abundance of energy. Hooked on his belt was an impressive ring, heavy with several dozen keys. He methodically tried the lot of them, one by one by one by one … on each machine in succession, until satisfied that *none* of them would open *anything*. Shrugging his shoulders, he slide-stepped over to the cooler showcasing the mystery sandwiches, swung open the front, and gestured for me to take what I wanted. They were pretty small and would have to hold me for at least another ten hours, so I picked out two that looked no worse than the rest. The young man took a swig from his bottle of Mountain Dew, replaced the cap, and dragged the back of his free hand across his mouth, before extending it palm up in my direction.

"Quince pesos cada uno por favor." ("Fifteen pesos (about two dollars) for each one, please.")

"¿Qué es?" *I should probably at least ask what they are …*

"Tortas ahogadas." ("Drowned sandwiches.")

Shit. I don't know what either word is. "¿Qué carne?" *I hope I'm asking what kind of meat it is.*

"¡Sí! Carne de cerdo." ("Yes! Pork meat.")

"Gracias." *Well, … I recognized "sí" and "carne." Maybe "torta" is some kind of pudgy tortilla. Lord only knows what that "day-seer-dough" thing is.*

"De nada."

No worries? Hah. Easy for you to say.

Still not knowing exactly what lay inside the wrapped packages in my hands, I handed over thirty pesos to close the deal. Careful not to drink from the water fountain, and unable to secure a soda from the machine, I was left with only my pair of mystery sandwiches for dinner.

I suppose it could best be described as a mixture of an oily French dressing, and perhaps … a briny tomato sauce, that oozed from the soggy rolls when the scotch tape and cellophane restraints were released. Now unsealed, they gave off a distinctly tangy aroma. Before taking a bite, I felt the need to ask someone if they were okay to eat. The ticket lady had been helpful, but a square of tattered cardboard, tucked behind the bars of her booth's window, ruled out that option for now. The kid had returned to carefully re-test each of his keys in the vending machines, still chasing the satisfaction a match would bring. I got his attention and passed one of the burnt-reddish, dripping handfuls near my face, scrunching up my nose and shaking my head in the universal language of "this stinks." He waved me over, keeping his other hand firmly on the key ring, apparently afraid to lose his place.

"Son un poco viejas, pero estoy seguro de que están bien." ("Those are a little old, but I'm sure they're okay.")

"Seguro" and "bien" are his only words I understand. "Sure" and "good."

"Lo siento, amigo. ¿'Seguro' and 'bien?'" *Is he saying these are okay to eat?*

Rubbing his stomach, "¡Sí! Me comí una hace un par de días. ¡Fue muy bueno!" ("Yes! I had one a couple of days ago. It was very good!")

I managed to choke down a couple of bites before deciding I might be better served by going hungry. Lacking anything to drink, or rinse my mouth with, a stubborn tang preyed upon me as I climbed aboard the bus bound for Mexico City two hours later. The bus was packed; the only open seat was on the aisle of the last row at the rear. My seatback didn't recline because it rested against the engine compartment behind me. A co-driver's bed was tucked into a compartment above the engine. A tiny restroom occupied the space where there would've otherwise been another pair of seats across the aisle from me. It wasn't but a few minutes after we left the Guadalajara station that every person on the bus, except for me and the old guy in the window seat next to me, had their shades down, overhead lights out, and seatbacks blissfully reclined.

Scheduled for seven nonstop hours, the ride began uneventfully. The highway was modern, and by Mexican standards, fairly straight and smooth. With all of the side windows blacked out by drawn shades, my only glimpse of the world outside was the glint from the occasional oncoming headlights that swept the interior of the bus like the beam of a distant lighthouse. An hour into the trip, the hypnotic tranquility this long stretch of highway presented was rapidly being eclipsed by a growing turbulence in my gut. *Goddammit. I knew I shouldn't have taken a bite of that thing; and I damn sure shouldn't have swallowed it!*

For the next few hours, I spent most of my time occupying the seat in the closet across the aisle, interrupted only when a fellow prisoner on the bus needed to use the facilities, far too sick to fret much about anyone having to follow me into that claustrophobic den. Crazed with fever and pretty certain I was going to die, my teeth chattered, my skin burned, and my clothes sagged heavy with sweat. My shoelaces no longer tied evidenced an aborted attempt to remove my pants and rid myself of soiled underwear. The old guy, once seated next to me, now sat cross-legged on the hard floor of the aisle at the front of the bus. Other than him, the driver, and myself, I assumed no one else stirred. Not that it mattered. It wasn't like anyone aboard would dare risk contact and offer me a blanket or a drink of water; and I didn't blame them. And now that my wristwatch belonged to a dump truck driver in La Ticla, I had no way to know how long I'd been on this bus, or, more importantly, how much longer until I could escape it.

My nose and throat burned—a byproduct of vomiting. Even so, the distinctive pungency of a long-dormant electric heater, switched on for the first time since spring, penetrated my senses.

Thank God! The driver's finally turning on the heat. You could hang meat in here.

My relief was short-lived. The odor, growing much sharper, was that of an electrical fire, and it was coming from the engine compartment behind my seat!

Maybe it's nothing. I could be delirious or hallucinating or something, right? Nope. Now there's smoke, too. *You've got to be kidding me …*

Dark, black, eye-watering smoke began flowing in earnest into the cabin from behind my seat, invading the space between me and the restroom, seeping past the curtain, drawn closed across the co-driver's compartment. A rush of adrenaline cleared my cobwebs. I jumped up, yanked aside the curtain, and woke him from a patently deep slumber.

"Fire! Fire! The engine is on fire!" *He's got to understand this, right?*

Rubbing his eyes, he mumbled, "¿Qual es tu problema?" ("What's your problem?")

His eyes flew wide open, "¡Oh mierda! ¡Mierda! ¡¡¡Mierda!!!" ("Oh shit! Shit! Shit!!!")

Wearing only black socks, sweatpants, and a wife beater T-shirt, he vaulted feet first out of his berth and sprinted to the front of the bus.

Hmmm… I guess "mierda" is how you say "fire" in Spanish.

The bus slowed quickly to a stop on the side of the highway, and I figured I'd do my part to help in any way I could. Jostling the passengers awake in the aisle seats of the rows in front of me, I declared in a loud, stern voice, commanding as much attention as possible,

"¡Mierda! ¡Mierda!" and pointed toward the rear of the bus.

The old woman seated directly in front of me didn't look up, or even open her eyes. Instead, she extended her middle finger in my direction and snarled,

"¡Cállate, pendejo!" *Okay. I learned this one in elementary school.* ("Shut up, asshole!")

"No, no! ¡Mierda Señora! ¡Mierda!" I recoiled to avoid the back of her hand, but she saw the smoke advancing along the floor and broke off her assault, mid-swing.

"¡Estamos en llamas!" She jabbed a finger into the ribs of the man asleep next to her. "¡Estamos en llamas!" ("We are on fire!")

An animated ripple of activity grew in intensity as it rolled forward, row by row, until cresting at the front of the bus as a minor tsunami. Passengers stirred, stood, adjusted their clothing, and gathered their belongings like we'd arrived at the station and were preparing to disembark. The co-driver was first off (still in his wife beater, sweatpants, and black socks) and carrying a fire extinguisher. Moments later, the sound of the engine hatch swinging open preceded a sustained *ba-whoooooosh!* from the extinguisher. The uniformed driver, still anchored behind the steering wheel, clicked on the PA and delivered a brief statement, not a word of which I understood. The primary point of his announcement became obvious as the line of sleepy passengers toddled forward: Everyone had to exit the bus.

The co-driver, still in his stocking feet and unable to cope with the cold outside any longer, pushed back in, past the line of passengers now halfheartedly leaving the bus. His nose deep red—bordering on purple—he was rubbing both arms vigorously and doing his utmost to deflect the grumbling,

"Lo siento. Lo siento. ¡Hace mucho frio por ahi!" ("I'm sorry. I'm sorry. It's very cold out there.")

This wasn't looking good for me. My long-sleeved T-shirt was soaked with sweat and clinging to the skin of my arms, back, and chest. Unprepared for anything other than the promised tropical warmth at the coast, the closest thing I had to cold-weather gear was a lightweight sweatshirt, which at this moment was cozily stowed in my backpack under the bus. Uncountable stars against a blacker-than-black sky, and a wall of obscenely cold air, overpowered my senses with my first footfall on the roadside. It was a merciless cold. A penetrating kind of cold I'd never experienced before.

The uniformed driver shepherded us to a patch of bare ground in front of the bus, but well off to the side of the divided highway. The headlights of our bus still shone brightly, making it impossible to see anything but them in that direction. Our shadows reached a sign barely discernable in the distance in front of us, a road sign we should have long since passed by.

San Cayetano Morelos
Elevación de 2.610 metros

Holy shit. That's like ... 8,500 feet! Explains why I'm well on my way to freezing to death out here ... Holy shit.

The co-driver emerged from the bus wearing a heavy coat and mittens. He whistled to get our attention and made an announcement—again, one completely lost on me—and met with more grumbling. Within a very few minutes, another bus (also emblazoned with "Tres Estrellas de Oro") pulled off the highway and slowed to a stop near our group.

Hallelujah! We're saved! THANK YOU GOD!

Our co-driver was welcomed aboard and engaged in a short conversation with the driver of our four-wheeled life raft. Rejoining our group two minutes later, he called three of the women to him and escorted them over to the new bus. A moment later, the doors clamped shut and our rescuer pulled away—all that remained was a cloud of diesel fumes and dust hanging in the air.

That's it? Three lousy people? How long until the next bus? There must be another forty-five of us out here! At this rate, some of us are sure to suffer the same fate as the Donner Party!

And so it went. Every ten to fifteen minutes another Tres Estrellas de Oro bus pulled off the highway, and anywhere from one to five people from our group climbed aboard and disappeared. Suffering unrelenting shaking, and intermittent dry heaves periodically augmented by bouts of diarrhea, I worried I'd become collateral damage to the breakdown. One hour passed; then a second and a third ... until only the co-driver, me, and our disabled bus remained. I pleaded with him to let me snag my pack, or get back aboard the bus, but through sign language, he insisted we stay out in the open where the passing buses could see us.

I didn't believe it could get any colder, but with the sky beginning to show signs of daybreak, the breeze picked up, and it did. Having grown too weak to stand any longer, I sat in a tight ball—arms embracing knees—on the frozen ground. It tested every ounce of rapidly fading willpower I had left to keep from tipping over.

I don't really know how long I'd been sitting there when the co-driver rousted me and helped me to my feet. My arms wouldn't work right and I couldn't feel my legs, so he pulled me up by my armpits and half-carried me to our rescue bus. It took two men to get me up the steps, and once inside, I learned there were no empty seats. I'd be relegated to sitting on the floor at the back of the bus. That was actually probably the best place for me to be, anyway. I was mercifully given a blanket, curled into the fetal position, and passed out.

Dead to the world around me, my dreams were bizarre. I dreamt that two policemen pulled me from the bus, walked me outside into blinding daylight, and pushed me into the back seat of an old Volkswagen Bug. We scooted along crowded streets; streets awash in a sea of colorful VWs. 'Round and 'round we went, orbiting a grand statue (with arms outstretched) anchoring the center of a chaotic solar system. We escaped its gravitational pull, only to be sucked into another, and then another. Our Bug came to a stop, and an upturned palm extended toward me from where the driver should be. I handed over my wallet; the driver walked me to an open door—pushed me inside—and left.

CHAPTER 10

THE ESCAPE

Carried by angels

The back of a soft hand gently brushed across my forehead and I blinked open my eyes.

"You've been asleep for thirty hours. How do you feel?"

"Where am I?" *It's the face of an angel looking back at me— but I'm laid out on an old mattress on the floor of a tiny and ordinary room, so it must not be heaven, right?*

"Mexico City. In my boyfriend's apartment near the university. My cousin, Salvador, delivered you here in his taxi yesterday. The police told him it was important to you to go to the university, but then you passed out and couldn't tell anyone *who* it was that you knew here."

Lifting the bedsheet, I didn't recognize the sweatshirt I was wearing. "You speak wonderful English. Where are my clothes?"

"My boyfriend is here for the study of earthquakes. He is from Alaska. He is teaching me English. As for your clothes, well, you arrived in the condition of a ... *un borracho callejero* ... let me see ... it's something like ... a typical bum from the gutter, I think."

"It's good that you are an American and knew to come to the university, or you might be in a real gutter now, and still wondering where you are."

"Thank you so much! I really don't remember a thing about how I got here. … I was very sick from some bad food … I think … from the bus station in Guadalajara." *She truly was an angel. Or maybe I was still dreaming?*

"Am I still dreaming? What is your name?"

"Isabela. My boyfriend, his name is Matthew. He calls me Izzy."

"I'm so sorry to forget my manners. My name is Paul. Paul Adam Wilson." No point whatsoever in divulging "Opters."

"Oh, we already discovered your name from your wallet." She pointed to my freshly laundered shirt and pants, neatly folded and stacked atop my tennis shoes beside the mattress, my wallet on top, ringed by my belt. I fight the urge to reach for it, realizing how totally uncool it would be for me to count my cash in front of her.

Isabela must have sensed my concern. She bit her lip, cocked her head a little, and gave me a very serious look, "Please Señor Paul. Please forgive me for peeking." She let that hang in the air for an extended moment, before raising one eyebrow and breaking into a mischievous grin. "You have a *lot* of money in your wallet for un borracho callejero. You must have some very big plans for here!"

"Hah! I wish I had big plans! I came to Mexico City to buy some parts for my Volkswagen Bus, which is broken down in Colima. I'm also hoping to find a camera shop that can repair my movie camera. You see, my Bus and my camera were caught up in a flash flood in a little town near Tecomán on the coast. This trip has been a total disaster for me so far." *What a dumbass … I'd better say something to soften that a bit!* "If not for the kind and honest people like you, I don't know if I would have survived it!"

Just then, the boyfriend arrived home, temporarily saving me from digging my hole any deeper.

Isabela called to him, "Matthew! He is awake! Paul is awake now!"

Matthew appeared to be Hawaiian or possibly Polynesian, I guessed. For some reason, I had expected him to be some rugged, red-bearded, direct descendant of the Vikings or something. I mean, him being from Alaska and everything. That nonfactor aside, Matthew had one of the warmest and most genuine demeanors of anyone (besides my mom) whom I'd ever met.

Isabela excused herself to prepare dinner, leaving Matthew and me to talk. He wanted to know everything about my trip, right down to the obscure details, details that I was positive would bore most anyone else. I told of the thirty-eight quarts of oil required to reach La Paz, and how incredible the people at the VW dealership there had been. I recounted how the "Red Sea of Cattle" had parted to let us through unharmed. He'd followed Hurricane Norman in the news, and couldn't believe we'd ridden it out aboard a ferryboat in the open ocean. I even described how we had used the swing of Moose's towel to calculate the height of the swells. A geological engineer, he loved it. Matthew marveled over our Ostula river crossings; one successful and the second, not so much. He said the region around Ostula had recently become *ground zero* in a deadly war between the farmers and the narco-terrorists, both seeking control of the fertile acreage in the Sierra foothills. Having mostly focused on the challenges of our trip to this point, I felt compelled to go ahead and tell him about the misdeeds each of us had committed prior to leaving, and wondered aloud if they could be a force behind our troubles somehow.

The three of us held hands at the table before digging into dinner. Matthew glanced my way, inferring an invitation to say grace, but I looked away just as quickly, hoping to throw it back to him. His prayer was beautiful. A loving expression of heartfelt appreciation to God, first for our trials, and then for the lessons learned, and finally for the security and peace in knowing *His* unwavering love for us.

Matthew and Isabela arranged for her cousin Salvador to pick me up in the morning. He'd take me to the off-road VW specialty parts-house, the camera repair shop, and return me to the main bus terminal downtown in time for my overnight trip back to Colima.

Matthew pulled me aside after dinner. "Paul, I've got to tell you three very important things. First: Salvador doesn't make much money, and he will never ask, but I know he didn't collect anything to bring you here from the bus station yesterday. I think ten or twelve dollars U.S. is good to add to whatever his fare is for tomorrow's errands. Second: Try hard to keep God in your heart. *He* is always with you. If you have faith in *His* mercy and *His* forgiveness, then draw a line on your past and leave your former ways behind you. And third: We only washed your *clothes*. You, however, still reek, and badly need a shower. I'm certain that Salvador, and your fellow bus passengers, will appreciate it. Good night."

De nada

Salvador was already sitting at the kitchen table and drinking coffee from an insulated tumbler by the time I'd finished putting on my shoes. Two days earlier, we'd shared an hour-plus drive in his VW Bug, a ride culminating with him physically carrying me to Matthew and Isabela's doorstep. This morning I was meeting him for the first time—my first while conscious and coherent, anyway.

Isabela greeted me with, "¡Buenos dias, Pablo! Este es mi primo, Salvador. El qué te trajo aqui desde la estacion de autobuses."

"Huh?"

"We're just messing with you, my friend! You looked lost again for a moment!"

They all shared a good laugh (at my expense) before Matthew stood. "Paul, this is Izzy's cousin Salvador. He's the one who brought you here from the bus station the other day. Salvador is also studying English, and doing very well."

I extended my hand. "Thank you, Salvador. My gosh, 'Thank you!' seems so feeble, after what you did for me."

He pulled me in for a quick hug and slap on the back. "¡De nada, Pablo! I am happy to have helped. You were in bad condition. I understand the rest, but what is, 'feeble?'"

"My friend, feeble means, 'weak,' or 'lacking strength.' You know, like I was when you helped me. But this time it describes how small my 'thank you' is, compared to what you did for me."

"De nada, Pablo." There it was again. "*De nada.*" Like a gigantic punctuation mark—one whose sole purpose is to keep the recipient from uttering another word.

I learned a new word at breakfast; two words, actually. *Pan dulce.* The four of us had pan dulce for breakfast, the same assortment of sweet rolls and pastries the young vendor had delivered to our dry-docked, cab-over camper in Colima each morning. One last coffee and it was time to go. We shared hugs and goodbyes, replete with plenty of "thank yous" and "de nadas." Isabela had packed me a lunch to eat on the bus ride back to Colima—"Because I obviously didn't have the good sense to avoid bus station food!"

Salvador reintroduced me to his faded lime-green and primer-gray VW Bug. Conspicuously missing the front passenger seat, it had been modified to serve as a taxicab. It was stripped of its headliner, armrests, visors, and floor mats. The traditional pair of vinyl-coated "passenger assist" strap handles had been replaced with sturdy, galvanized-steel, garage door handles. Noticing my interest in them, Salvador smiled and said,

"We call those, '¡Oh Dios mío! manijas' down here. 'Oh my God! handles.' They can be very useful in the city, especially in the traffic circles downtown."

Getting the engine rings was the whole reason for my trip to Mexico City, and Salvador took me to get them first. No problem at all; they knew exactly what I needed and had them in stock. We were in and out in under five minutes, four new rings in hand. It felt very unsatisfying and incomplete to me. I mean: the bus ride from hell, being so sick, the fire, nearly freezing to death, two days and nights at Matthew and Isabela's, another marathon bus ride yet to come ... *The climax of it all, five minutes in an auto parts store???*

"You look sad, Paul. Aren't you happy they had the right parts for you?"

That obvious, eh? "No, I'm happy to finally have the parts. It just feels very anticlimactic after everything."

"Perhaps you came here for another reason, Paul?"

Well, that cut me. It's all about me again, and I'm showing it.

"I'm sorry, Salvador. I didn't mean it like that. It's just that so many things—both good things and bad things—have happened to me in the last few days that, what I expected to be the most important part of this trip to Mexico City, has become the least of it. I'm very sure I will treasure the kindness your family has shown me, long after my troubles have been forgotten."

"De nada."

Next stop was across town to a camera repair shop owned by Salvador and Isabel's uncle Jorge. Matthew had told me that it was the best place in all of Mexico to have my movie camera repaired, and he would see to it that it was shipped back to me when it was ready. The storefront was modern and impressive, with a large and intricately woven, neon tube sign over the entrance:

REPARACION DE ARTICULOS FOTOGRAFICOS Y CINEMATROGRAFICOS EN GENERAL
Jorge M. Espejel,
Propietario

Wow. What a blessing to have hooked up with this clan! Everything I've needed is available within the family!

"Wow, Salvador. You have a family that can do everything!"

"Pablo, in Mexico our family is very important to us. This tradition … or value … extends across many generations. We are taught to honor and respect all of them." He continued with a smile, "Even the ones who may not deserve it so much. I won't be taking you for a visit with my uncle who resides in our Prisión Estatal… our State Prison. But he, too, is family. And we learn from a very young age to honor all who share our blood."

That's pretty cool. Personally, I think I'd run out of "family" I've met, before I'd run out of fingers to count 'em on.

Jorge looked over my movie camera and carefully removed a panel from the bottom of it, revealing the electronics packed inside were caked in mud still damp enough to glisten under his workbench light. He looked sad, like a veterinarian examining a pet that wasn't going to survive an encounter with a car. Jorge removed my twelve small boxes of exposed film from the bag, excused himself, entered a room near a back corner of his shop, and closed the heavy door behind. Five minutes passed before he returned, again looking a bit forlorn.

He turned to Salvador and rattled off a few sentences in Spanish. I didn't understand much of it, but his demeanor and his gestures confirmed my worst fears. My brand-new, top-of-the-line, Nikon XL8S Super-8 movie camera with power zoom telephoto lens, slow motion, freeze frame ... *the one I'd always wanted* ... was toast.

Salvador started to relay the bad news to me in English, but I put up my hand. "I understood enough. The camera cannot be saved, right?"

"No. I'm sorry my friend. My uncle says it is a total loss. Your film is bad, too. He examined it in his darkroom. Every roll has been exposed to water, and is ruined."

Thank God my mom had insisted I bring her old drugstore brand Pocket Instamatic along, or no one would believe any of this had really happened.

Jorge carefully replaced the side panel of the camera, returned it and the ruined film to the bag and reverently set it all back on the counter in front of me. "Lo siento, señor."

"De nada, señor. De nada. Thank you for checking it for me."

Salvador bailed me out, turning to his uncle and translating: "Gracias por comprobarlo por mi."

"De nada."

Deemed worthless, my fancy camera and the twelve rolls of my exotic "filmed on location" surf movie stayed behind with Jorge (one less thing to lug around, I suppose), and we headed off to the main bus terminal downtown. The station was a chaotic place. I couldn't believe I was walked to the curb by police officers and unceremoniously deposited into Salvador's taxi here a couple of days ago. Out of the scores of taxicabs here, I ended up in this one. *Thank you, God.* He retrieved my backpack from the front and met me at the curb.

"Thank you, Salvador. How much is my fare?" (He'd been carting me around for a couple of hours by now.)

"Is 150 pesos okay? That's about twenty dollars U.S."

I pulled forty dollars from my wallet and handed it to him, "No. Twenty dollars is not enough. Please accept this. I wish I had ten times this amount to give to you. Thank you for everything, my friend. And before you can say anything back to me, ... De nada."

Jugolandia dowry

The Tres Estrellas de Oro bus ride back to Colima was awesome. Although both buses were completely full, I scored a window seat on each, and when I wasn't sleeping, I filled my time staring at the amazing star-filled skies. I looked around the Guadalajara station during our short layover and bus change there. I didn't see the kid (the one with the two-liter Mountain Dew buzz on) who sold them to me, but the display case full of mystery sandwiches still was there. I didn't get within ten feet of it. Been there. Done that.

Upon arrival in Colima early the next morning, the town square was alive with activity. Several groups of school-age children were horsing around, waiting for their buses to arrive. The boys wore crisp-collared shirts and black trousers; the girls, white blouses and dark, plaid-patterned skirts. I recognized the dress code as that of Catholic school kids, and this morning the kids looked like they were off to somewhere or something especially important.

I expected a "school-bus yellow" bus to stop and pick up the kids, but the one that pulled up was blue and white—complete with a border of white dingle balls ringing the windshield. It *was* an old school bus. A *very old* one. A classic really, that had been reincarnated as a city transit bus. And it was the bus I'd been directed to take to the VW dealership. A rush of tittering girls, all in their matching uniforms, swarmed the door, leaving me surrounded as the lone adult in the group. Feeling more than a little awkward, I retreated a few steps and watched the bus fill to capacity without me. The only one yet to board, I gave the driver a questioning look.

He beckoned me over and asked, "¿A dónde vas?"

I knew this one. "Volkswagen." *Hope that's enough direction; that's all I have.*

He waved me aboard and motioned for me to go to the rear. I was at least half a foot too tall for the ceiling in the bus, and my head was bracketed by twin runs of a galvanized-pipe handhold—evidently pretty darn amusing to the busload of school girls. Scrunching down to clear the ceiling, and dragging my backpack along behind me, elicited a faux scream and panicked squeal from the back,

"¡El es Frankenstein!" ("He is Frankenstein!")

The bus erupted into a cacophony of screams, laughter, and choruses of "Frankenstein!" "Frankenstein!" "Frankenstein!" It was hysterical. I couldn't resist playing along a bit, kicking my left foot forward stiffly, dragging my right foot (splayed outward) along behind me, and very slowly making my way to the back.

The driver must have been watching the show in his mirror, or worse, over his shoulder. The bus drifted to the right and our tires clipped a curb. A violent twist of the chassis raced from front to back, every head onboard snapping first right and then left. Mine was pinballed between the two galvanized-pipe handholds running the length of the ceiling. I was dropped like a sack of wet cement. Out cold.

I'm not sure how long I was out, but it was long enough for the bus driver to be kneeling over me when I opened my eyes. Helping me to my feet, he walked me to the front of the bus, guided me down the steps and out the open door.

Is he getting rid of the evidence? Now what?

He called to a young woman, stationed behind the counter of a juice stand across the street. They exchanged a few sentences before I was handed off to her care, and the bus pulled away. She had me sit on one of the half dozen or so bar stools that spanned the length of the counter, dumped ice (a half scoop each) into two dish towels, rolled them up, and had me hold one against either side of my head. That completed, she went about preparing and serving me an incredible, fresh papaya-banana-orange-egg-coconut-honey smoothie. I was infatuated. With the smoothie, I mean.

Having had my bell rung hard (twice!), I welcomed the opportunity to sit there with bags of ice on my head and a frozen delight in front of me. I wondered if a case of brain freeze might actually be a good thing under the circumstances, and took another long, deep, drag from my straw.

"¡Gracias! ¿Cómo te llamas?" *All credit goes to Mr. Brown's eighth-grade Spanish class for that.* ("Thank you! What is your name?")

"Mi nombre es Rosa. ¿Y usted?" ("My name is Rosa. And yours?")

"Mi nombre es Pablo. ¡Hola Rosa, mucho gusto!" *See Mr. Brown? I was paying attention!* ("My name is Paul. Hello Rosa, I'm pleased to meet you!")

"Igualmente."

Okay, I don't know that one, but it sounded like a good thing. I'll just nod and smile.

Finished with the smoothie, I figured this was a good time to get my bearings and sort out where I was in relation to the VW dealership. I leaned back far enough to make out the colorful signage over the juice shop counter.

"Jugolandia." Wow! What a perfect name for this place! "Juice Land." I literally could *live* on the concoctions this place sells! Stepping out onto the sidewalk revealed I was across the street and only two blocks away from the VW dealership! The sooner I got these rings into their hands, the sooner we could get back on the road home. I pulled the package of engine parts from my pack and did a decent job of sign language, communicating to Rosa that I needed to take them down the street to the VW mechanics.

Rosa and her father, Eduardo, working the counter
at "Jugolandia" in Colima, Colima.

"¿Cuánto cuesta, Rosa?" *Oops. Moose taught me that one. I hope to God, it doesn't only apply to prostitutes!*
"De nada, Pablo."
Again?! I can't accept this with no charge! Good grief! I'll drop the parts at VW, come back here, and try again.

The dealership was another nonissue situation. The service manager checked the rings I'd brought him for my engine and told me my Bus would be ready by tomorrow afternoon. Yee-haw!!! I leaned in and raised my hand, planning to exchange a high five with him; but he seemed more bored than anything, dismissing me with a single, halfhearted chin-bob.

Back at Jugolandia, Rosa introduced me to her father, Eduardo, who apparently owned the shop. Beneath the brim of his cowboy hat, Eduardo's face looked weathered and weary, a victim of way too many days in the tropical sun. He insisted I sit on a stool at the center of the bar, and pulled up his own stool next to mine. In spite of his English being every bit as limited as my Spanish, we did our best to communicate, and actually did a pretty fair job of it. He had Rosa prepare and serve me another smoothie. This one was more magical than the first, though I wasn't able to watch what all she'd put into it. I told him it was the best thing I'd ever tasted, and asked if he had other locations. He got the point across to me that this was the only one, and he'd spent more than thirty years behind this counter perfecting his recipes. He told me his sons didn't want anything to do with the business anymore, and his wife had passed away last year. Rosa was the youngest, his lone daughter and the only one to stay committed to the family business. With a sigh, he shared that she would be the one to inherit the stand when he grew too old to continue.

I was having such a good time—already on my third extra-large smoothie—and still talking with Eduardo. There was absolutely no need (and I had no desire) to rush back to the camper in the boonies and hang out with Moose and Jelly. With nothing pressing, and time to kill until tomorrow, I could relax and spend a while longer with my new friends. Time flew, and "regulars" came and went. All that was needed was some baseball on the old black and white television at the end of the bar, and this could've passed for a small-town watering hole just about anywhere.

A couple of hours later, and already approaching dusk, Eduardo invited me to go eat with him at his friend's restaurant nearby. Thumping my snare-drum tight stomach, I laughed and told him I was so obscenely bloated—having spent my day chain-drinking smoothies—there was no chance in hell I could eat anything more. I told him I'd really enjoyed my time with him and his daughter, and I would see him again tomorrow when I came for my Bus.

Pointing to the nearly empty smoothie cup in front of me, I held up four fingers,

"¿Cuánto cuesta, cuatro?" *I think I've polished off at least four of 'em … Oh my.*

Eduardo raised his index finger to his lips, signaling me to be quiet. *At least he's not saying,* "¡De nada!" *Come on, man. I need to pay for these.*

He motioned for me to step to the curb with him.

"¿Te gusta Rosa?"

I wasn't grasping where he was going with this.

"Pablo, Rosa está lista para casarse ahora." ("Paul, Rosa is ready to marry now.")

"Lo siento. No entiendo. I'm sorry, Eduardo. I don't understand."

Eduardo pointed to his wedding band, and then to Rosa, and then to me, and interlinked his two index fingers.

Oh shit. He wants me to marry Rosa!

My eyes must've been as big as saucers. I didn't know what to say, much less how to say it in Spanish, so I just stood there looking the fool.

"Pablo, es el sueño de Rosa vivir en América. Tengo dinero guardado para enviar con ella." ("Paul, it is Rosa's dream live in America. I have money saved to send with her.")

After a long and tortured mix of gestures, middle-school Spanish, and a pinch of English, I think Eduardo understood: I wanted to think it over tonight and I would give him my answer tomorrow. I walked back over to say good night to Rosa.

She is *pretty, and makes one helluva great smoothie ... I wonder if there is a back way into the VW service area?*

Leaving, I felt guilty; like I may have unwittingly scammed Jugolandia out of four of the world's best smoothies.

Ay-yay-yay!

"Rosa."

Back at the camper in the middle of nowhere, the first thing out of Jelly's mouth was, "Man you look like hell. Eat a sandwich or something!"

I just polished off four smoothies—and I still *look like a skeleton?*

"You were gone an extra day. Did you get the parts? When is that pig of yours going to be ready?" Moose, cutting to the chase.

"No hay problema. It'll be ready tomorrow afternoon."

My physique after losing the gastrointestinal grudge match to the Guadalajara bus station grub.

Jungle of Trouble, redux

There wasn't any grand, VW repair shop going-away ceremony this time. Just a, "Pay the bill, take the keys, and be on your way" kinda deal. Other than seeing (via the receipt) the engine had been pulled and dismantled for the third time in a month, you wouldn't have known the Bus had been touched since its swim in the Ostula River. They hadn't even bothered to clean the streaked mud from the inside of the windshield, making me suspicious they'd road tested the Bus when they were done. One particularly nice touch though, was the paper mat (emblazoned with two large, blue shoe prints and the VW service center logo) on the driver's side floor. Of course, it was lying *on top* of several inches of dried mud …

I felt a little conflicted, detouring off the main drag in order to avoid driving past Jugolandia on our way out of town. I'd made the mistake of sharing Eduardo's "marriage proposal" with the guys and, predictably, they'd reacted by developing an unquenchable thirst for smoothies, tormenting me with it at every opportunity.

It felt good to finally be on the road again, though it was breaking my heart to see the 1DRBUS so completely coated inside and out with dirt, nary a square inch undefiled. The shortest route home was closed due to a landslide, so we backtracked down the mountain and onto the coast highway once more—this time, heading north. Our plan was to stop for the night *before* entering the "Jungle of Trouble" again. Moose had actually been the one to suggest it, obviously still freaked out by the bat on our windshield (and, coincidentally, right after I'd recounted my conversation with the Anglo truck driver on our way south).

Though we'd had coffee with our breakfast, its caffeine seemed superfluous as we reentered the Jungle of Trouble the next morning. The three of us were wide awake, all eyes glued to the road and the jungle around us, on guard for the slightest indication of witch doctors or renegade cannibals.

Figuring I could tweak him a little: "Hey Moose, I wonder if a witch doctor's curse made the air vent moan like that our last time through here. I mean, it's never happened before or since, and I've never heard of it happening to anyone else."

"I don't know. That noise and that fucking bat. They messed with my head. I've had nightmares about it. Fuckin' creeps me out."

Moose, with nightmares? How funny!

"Yeah, Opters, open the vent and see if it'll do it again." asked Jelly.

"Sure. Sit close so you can hear it."

The lever (normally easy to operate) was stiff and stubborn. It wouldn't budge, so I adjusted my grip and put my weight into it. It broke free all at once and went from closed tight to max-open in an instant. It was as if someone had ambushed us. A half-dozen handfuls of burnt-red- clay dust exploded into our faces. A blinding, choking cloud filled the air. I couldn't see—could barely breathe. I stuck my head out the window, but with so much crap: coating my face, matting my hair, and scratching my eyes, it didn't help. It took a lot of luck to stay on the pavement and come to a stop. Not knowing (and frankly, not caring) where we were on the road at that moment, we bailed out like coal miners escaping a cave-in.

"What'd you do that, for?!" said Moose, bent at the waist, hands on knees, coughing, spitting dirt.

"How the fuck was I supposed to know that would happen?"

"Maybe it was your witch doctor, Moose. Yeah, that's the ticket! Ack-ack-ack-ack. Moose has his own personal witch doctor poking pins in him somewhere in the jungle, ack-ack-ack-ack!"

It took a few minutes for us to get on the road home again. We took turns dusting off each other's shoulders and backs, whisked the sticky red powder from our hair, and emptied all of the canteens into our eyes. I managed to return the vent lever to the off position. Nevertheless, we stuffed rags, socks, wads of paper, and whatever else we could find, into all of the louvers just to be sure.

Departing the jungle, the highway took us along the coast and bordered the waterfront in Puerto Vallarta. We spotted our ferry, moored at the same landing where we'd begun the mainland part of our trip, little more than three weeks earlier. Noting the line of cars and trucks being loaded for the next crossing, I wondered if they'd fixed the second engine yet.

The guys wanted to reach Mazatlán before stopping, but that would be another seven hours, on top of the four we'd already driven. Worn out, I only managed another five before making an executive decision to camp a couple of hours south of there for the night and get a fresh start in the morning.

No way to slow down

North out of Mazatlán, the highway straightened out, and stone-cold boredom set in. At our first gas stop, an old guy approached, asking if he could get a ride north. Since Moose and Jelly had taken to napping in the back, I welcomed the guy on board, reasoning he'd help me stay awake and pass the time. His name was Umberto, and we worked out that he'd begun his trek in Guatemala a week earlier (walking, mostly), his goal to reach "Los Estados Unidos." He'd left his wife and four sons behind—didn't know anyone willing to brave the long and uncertain journey with him, so he was going it alone. He didn't comprehend one lick of English, and his Spanish sounded different than any I'd heard before. I pointed to

Moose and Jelly (both still napping on the bed) in the back and said their names. He took one look at Moose, pointed to his head, and called him, "Hombre canche." (Mayan slang for "blondie man.")

"Hey Moose!" I said, deliberately waking him up. "Umberto here, says you are 'hombre canche.' What is that? *Sounds like 'girly man' to me.*"

"Fuck if I know. Why'd you pick up a hitchhiker?"

"Because I'm bored silly up here, and after denying the old couple a ride across the river in La Ticla, I figured my karma could use some help."

"Yeah? Where's he going?"

"All the way to Los Angeles, but we're only taking him as far as T.J. The rest is up to him."

I gave my new friend a thumbs-up and he smiled in return, exposing a mouthful of brutally bad teeth and sore-looking gums.

The day crawled, the heat and humidity oppressive, the scenery seldom varied; half desert scrub and half farmland, mile after mile after mile. It reminded me of Central California—same heat, noxious odors and dust—but with ten times the bugs and triple the humidity. The guys returned to napping (best they could) in the back. Umberto struggled to stay awake, his head leaning against the window. Every once in a while I tapped the brakes, just to keep everyone else on board, "in the game" with me.

It had been twenty minutes since we passed through the last small town ... and equally as long since turning the steering wheel was necessary. Without warning, the rear wheels locked up and sent the Bus into a skid. Instinctually, I slammed the clutch pedal to the floor, and the Bus began to roll normally again.

"Fucking knock it off, Opters!" Moose snarled, "Let us sleep, goddammit!"

"I didn't do that! I don't know what the hell happened. The back wheels locked up all of a sudden."

Letting the clutch out a little slowed the Bus, like pressing on the brakes, so I took it out of gear and tried it again. No problem.

"I think something's wrong with the transaxle. It acts like it seized or something. I need to stop and take a look at it." *This isn't feeling like it's going to be simple …*

Reprising their "seniors on a tour bus" routine from our first full day on the road a month ago, everyone stayed put while I got out to see what I could under the Bus. The pavement was hotter than a skillet, and the fruit flies must have watched us stop, because they swarmed my face the moment I lay down. It only took a second to know we were screwed; the transaxle was puffing steam and transmission oil was pulsing past a ruptured seal on the side. Steam could only mean one thing: Water got into the (supposedly factory-sealed) transaxle in the river. It turned to steam here on Hades Highway, the pressure blew out a seal—allowing the oil to escape—and now the rear end had seized up tighter than Moose's wallet.

"It's done, you guys. Transaxle is seized. Seals blew out. It's done."

"Now what, Opters?

"I don't know, Jelly. I really don't know. Get it to another dealer? Fuck, I don't know."

C'mon, God. I got your point a week ago when I was in Mexico City. "Don't mess with stuff that doesn't belong to you." I got it. Again, you're kicking my ass? Again?

I was as mentally beaten down as a person could possibly be. I'm not sure what "giving up" would consist of right now, or I'd be mulling it over.

"What was that last town we went through?"

"Guasave. Why, Moose?"

"'Cause we're gonna go get someone to tow this pig back there and find out if it can be fixed. Because if it can't be fixed—and I mean *fixed today*—I'm grabbing my shit and hitching a ride home without it, *or you*."

Not waiting for Jelly, "I'm with you, Moose. If it can't be fixed today, I'll leave this pig here. … I'm done."

Jelly and Umberto stayed with the Bus while Moose and I hitched a ride back to the last town we'd passed. It was midafternoon on a Sunday, and it had to be 115 in the shade. Guasave was a ghost town. We wondered if maybe it was some kind of Mexican holiday; not a single soul was out and about. Even the PEMEX was closed.

Fifteen minutes into our search for a sign of life, we came upon a couple of guys sitting on the hood of a white, four-door Chevy "Taxi" parked under a tree, drinking beers. Moose did his best to explain our situation and the need for a tow back to town. I'm not certain they understood we were asking for an actual tow truck, but at this point I'd ceded everything over to Moose. They said they could tow us back for forty dollars, and had the perfect rope to do it with. That would leave a sum total of twenty-seven dollars remaining between the three of us. But really: What were our other options? We didn't have much of anything left to barter with (surfboards just aren't a high-demand commodity in the desert). Before committing, I asked to see the rope. They obliged, pulling the end of it from the trunk to show me. Thick as my arm, it looked like an anchor rope from the *Queen Mary*. The deal done, the four of us climbed into the taxi for the ride back to where the 1DRBUS had broken down.

"Man, what took you guys so long? We thought maybe you were on that Tres Estrellas de Oro bus to Mexicali that went by a while ago! Where's the tow truck?"

"Sorry, Jelly. The whole town was shut down for some kind of holiday or something. It took forever to find someone. This is Joaquín and Angel; they're gonna tow us back to Guasave."

We hadn't yet worked out exactly *where* in Guasave we were being towed to, but off this highway was a good start.

Our new friends backed their Chevy up to the Bus and produced the rope. It was only about six feet long! Yes, it *was* as thick as my arm, but six feet long?!

"Where's the rest of the rope? Moose, ask 'em where the longer rope is. This one's way too short. Once we tie it to both cars, there won't be two feet between us!" *They've got to be messing with me, right?*

Moose talked it over with them for a minute. "That's it, Opters. That's their rope. They said they use it for this kind of thing all the time, and not to worry. It used to be longer, but they gave some of it to another taxi last week."

"Seriously? Okay. Let me think. Is there some kind of knot that doesn't use up much rope?" *This is insane.*

"Hey. Me and Jelly are going to ride in the taxi. You and your buddy can hang out in the Bus."

Yeah, sure Moose. You guys go ahead and relax with your chauffer up there, while me and Umberto do our best not to die.

"Yeah, Opters. That's the ticket! You guys take the Bus. The bus ticket. Get it? Ack-ack-ack-ack."

I'm not in the mood, Jelly.

The guys made themselves comfortable in the back seat of the Chevy while Ángel tied one end of the rope to their bumper, leaving a bit over three feet of it for me. Unable to tie an actual knot at my end (and still leave a gap between our cars) I used a bolt and some wire to lash my end of the rope to the Bus. I redid the knot under the taxi and gained another few inches, leaving us a net distance of about a foot and a half between his trunk and my headlights. Sitting behind my steering wheel, I couldn't see the rear of his car, only the top of his trunk.

"¿Estás listo, Umberto? … Are you ready?"

He turned to me, eyes wide, and paused a few seconds before answering with a jittery nod.

Pulling onto the highway, I could tell it was going to be tricky maintaining the space between our vehicles. Drift a little to one side or the other, and the angle of the rope drew us closer yet. I'd need to anticipate them slowing, and apply my brakes ever so lightly, to keep us from "kissing." Because the highway was divided along this stretch, we had to drive north a few miles before we could cross over and head back south to Guasave. We started out at about twenty-five miles an hour, and I was cool with that as long as they didn't make any sudden course or speed changes.

"No problema, Umberto?"

"Sin problema."

He had both hands locked onto the dashboard grab handle in front of him, still looking concerned. We negotiated the overpass and entered the southbound side of the highway without an issue, although our speed was picking up a little.

"Mira. Fuman mota." Umberto got my attention and motioned to the rear window of the Chevy. ("Look. Smoking pot.")

"Unbelievable. Are you fucking kidding me?!"

The guys were passing a joint around. Jelly held the doobie up to the rear window for me to see, and Moose flashed a thumbs-up, both of them wearing Cheshire cat grins.

Dear God, I hope it's Commercial-wa-khan dirt-weed and not some kick-your-ass stuff!

Our speed continued to creep up, passing forty now. With them stoned, I prayed they'd go slower, but in reality, they may have forgotten we were back here. We passed an eighty km/h sign, and I knew it translated to about fifty mph; the speedometer read sixty. We were speeding, and drifting side to side. Okay, this was getting to be a bit much.

"Esto es muy peligroso."

"Yeah, Umberto. Sí, muy peligroso."

The spider in El Faro was muy peligroso! Umberto is hairing-out on this right along with me.

I didn't know exactly what to do about it. I tapped the brakes, thinking it may get their attention, but nothing. Shit! We hit seventy! Fuck this. I pumped the brakes hard a couple times, hoping I could break loose from them somehow, but I couldn't create enough slack to give the rope a hard yank, and I wasn't sure they even noticed. I leaned on my horn, let up, and leaned on it again. Just then, we passed by two Federales standing in front of a Highway Patrol car in the shade of an overpass on the other side of the road. My honking garnered their attention, and they scrambled to get back in their car.

Moose turned and glared at me. Jelly did an exaggerated version of the universal signal for "shush!" Joaquin? He punched it. Past seventy-five; touching eighty; then my speedometer pegged at eighty-plus mph. (Yeah, yeah. I've heard all about it. *You* ride in a '66 VW Bus going eighty and tell me it should go faster.) The Highway Patrol car had crossed the median and was in hot pursuit—lights flashing, siren blaring! I was a 1000 percent focused on not screwing up. Joaquin not only was hauling ass, he was changing lanes back and forth, cutting through traffic. (It's funny how "light traffic" feels so much more congested, when you're going twice as fast as it is.) My Bus felt like a rag doll in a toddler's hand. It literally was *everything* I could do to keep all four wheels on the ground, avoid fishtailing, and not bump the back of the Chevy.

There was growing congestion in front of us. Traffic was backing up, and we'd have to slow down … Wouldn't we? No, I guess not. Onto the left shoulder—we're traveling at least sixty mph faster than the cars and trucks in the fast lane beside us. The Highway Patrol trailed by about two hundred yards and closing. I saw the reason for the backup up ahead: There was an old farm tractor *quadruple-towing* propane trailers behind it in a single, long, serpentine *train*. A train that was snaking back and forth—from shoulder to shoulder across both lanes—like Puff (Boom?) the Magic Freaking Dragon!

Like he'd done this a dozen times before, Joaquín timed it perfectly, dipped in and out of the oscillating wave, staying with it until we were safely past the tractor. I looked in the mirror and watched the Highway Patrol break off the chase, obviously considering the risk of passing the deadly serpent too dangerous to continue. Not ready to claim victory just yet, Joaquín continued up the highway (my speedometer still pegged past eighty) for another few miles. Without warning, he slowed to fifty and veered off the right shoulder onto the native earth of the highway frontage. We were linked so closely behind the Chevy, I couldn't see the holes, ruts, rocks, and ditches lacing the ground in front of us, but did my best to mimic his swerves. I suppose I missed a direct hit on a few of them; it's hard to say. We bottomed through several so violently as to ricochet Umberto off the ceiling on his way to my lap, my co-pilot gamely never letting go of his dash-mounted grab handle.

We made a hard right turn off the frontage and onto a two-rut-trail that took us into a patch of low trees where we stopped in a cloud of dust. So furious I could hardly breathe, I jumped out from behind the wheel and bull-rushed the driver's door. Jelly's door swung into my path to slow me.

"Wait! Wait! He had to do it!" Jelly corralled me with his free arm.

Joaquín skirted us, moved quickly to the rear of the Chevy, popped open the trunk, and said, "¡Mira!," pointing into the trunk. "No podía frenar." ("Look! I couldn't slow down.")

There were no less than 150, blue-cellophane-wrapped bricks (each the size of a New York City phonebook laid on edge), organized into two neat layers and filling the trunk. *Holy shit.*

"Yeah, Opters. We couldn't stop or we'd have all gone to jail. A fucking Mexican jail!"

"No. Can't go to jail! Ack-ack-ack-ack. Can't go to jail!"

I was in a daze. "So how was the pot?" I think maybe I could use a little buzz myself about now.

"How'd your friend like the ride?"

"Shit, Jelly! I forgot all about him!"

The cars were too close to pass between, so I walked around the back of the Bus to get to Umberto's, still closed, door. Startled by the click of the latch, he snapped his head in my direction, eyes in an unfocused, fixed stare, past me. His stock-still hands clenched the dashboard grab handle in a white-knuckled death-grip. And he'd peed himself.

Umberto didn't say a word after that. Perhaps he was embarrassed, or for all intents and purposes, in shock. He didn't stick around long enough to determine. The last I saw of him, he was wobbling away from us in the general direction of the highway. I called out to him, "Vaya con Dios, Umberto!" but got nothing in return, not so much as a look back over his shoulder. (I wonder if he ever made it to Los Angeles—or turned around and went home.)

A load of chicken shit

We didn't expend much time or energy trying to find someone in Guasave who could fix the transaxle for us; it seemed likely an impossible task. Joaquín and Angel said we could leave the 1DRBUS with them—they would take it someplace for safekeeping—and we could return later with something able to tow it back to San Diego. I was skeptical it would be findable when, or if, I made it back. I'd lost everything. My spirit was broken. It almost didn't matter anymore if my Bus was here when I returned. I needed to go home.

None of us had enough cash remaining to afford a bus ticket to Tijuana from here. Even pooling it together, our money got only one of us home, and left nothing leftover to buy food for the two who stayed behind. We were just shy of nine hundred miles from Imperial Beach, and we were going to have to hitchhike (or walk) to get there. Moose and Jelly grabbed their boards and a canteen; me, an extra pair of socks, sunscreen, and mosquito repellent. I didn't bother with my board. I was too beaten down to care. Joaquín gave me the address and phone number of a friend, and I snapped a picture of the taxi—so I'd have a backup means, and half a shot of finding them again—when they dropped the three of us off on the side of the highway heading north out of town.

The trunk of Joaquín and Ángel's Taxi is
an image forever etched into my mind!

I used a pencil and the back of my repair bill from VW of Colima to make a sign to hold. I didn't know if anyone referred to Tijuana as "T.J." this far south, but that's all I could think to draw on it. We must've looked every bit as hapless and pathetic as we felt, standing out there in the blazing heat. None of us spoke a word. We just stood there with our thumbs out, watching truck after truck, and car after car full of people gawk as they drove on by.

"Fuck this. I'm gonna start walking. Nut'n to be gained by standing *here* any longer. Do me a favor. If someone picks you up, have 'em stop and gimme a ride, too. Okay?"

"Okay, Moose. We'll do that. I promise."

I'm not sure who was abandoning whom, right then, but the scene playing out before me of someone walking off into the desert—pursuing a mirage, while carrying a surfboard—made me close my eyes and hang my head in anguish.

Moose hadn't made it fifty feet, when a young couple driving a big, stake-bed truck, stacked high with cages, pulled off the highway. They said they were transporting a load of chickens to Mexicali, and if we wanted to rearrange the cages to create the space, they'd give us a ride all the way there. Five minutes later, we'd carved out just enough room among the chickens to fit two surfboards and the three of us, and we were on our way.

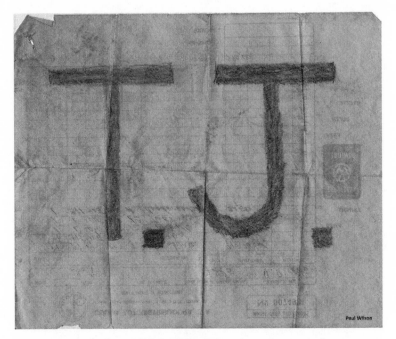

My receipt from VW de Colima was the only piece of paper
I could find to make a sign with.

To say it was brutal, pays short-shrift to brutal: Never-ending flurries of chicken feathers, the overpowering stench of their shit in the desert heat, sixteen hours on an old, splinter-laden sheet of plywood without room to lie down, and only one fifteen-minute stop for gas, between when we got on, and when we got off in Mexicali.

Was the driver being gracious, or getting even for something?

He *was* kind enough to point us in the direction of the Mexicali bus station, where we used all but four dollars of our remaining cash to purchase three tickets to Tijuana.

Saluting the end of this chapter ...
from the back of the chicken truck.

CHAPTER 11

GOING BACK FOR MORE

An overdue "Ed-u-ma-cātion"

Only a handful of people knew we were back, and the ones who did were sworn to secrecy. Moose certainly didn't want anyone to know. He was facing four years in jail for manslaughter—*plus* whatever they were going to tack on for hightailing it to Mexico on the morning he was supposed to have reported for confinement. I don't think Jelly was all that anxious to face Sherri right away, either. No amount of "Ack-ack-ack-ack" was going to get him out of that mess.

Me? I couldn't remember if I'd moved a muscle in hours. I stared at the ceiling, my head tipped back against the wall. My body, like so much dead weight, pressed deeply into the cushions of the old sofa in our living room. I hadn't done enough physically in the last thirty-plus days to merit feeling this tired, but even holding a can of beer seemed a chore. My energy was sapped, spent on a single objective, to work out a plan to get the 1DRBUS back home—*if* it was still in Guasave for the finding.

I'd racked my brain over who might be willing to tackle such a challenge as this with me. After all, *anyone* who knew *anything* about what had happened to us during the month we were in Mexico, had to assume we were cursed in some way; and who in their right mind wants to join a party of cursed souls? There was but one person who would even consider such foolishness: My roommate, and best friend, Perro, and he'd just walked in from work, grabbed a beer, and plopped down on the over-stuffed chair across from me.

"Hey Perro. Remember how easily your truck handled all of that shit we stole that night in Coronado?" I'll get him puffed up a bit, fawning over his three-quarter-ton, four-wheel drive Ford XLT 250. "You sure have one awesome truck there!" Laying it on thick, "You ever think about getting a travel trailer to haul behind it. I mean, you could tow pretty much anything you wanted with it, right?"

"Yeah. It's a killer truck, Opters; never given me a problem. Why? You want to buy it or something?"

I think he might be seeing through my bullshit.

"Nah, I can't afford to buy anything as nice as it right now. Not with my Bus stuck down in Mexico like it is. Hey … uh (like it just occurred to me) … would you consider helping me go get it? Tow it back here? I can pay you something."

Perro danced, searching for a graceful way out. "I can't do that, Opters! I can't afford to take that much time off work!"

Having anticipated his first salvo, I'd rehearsed my answer beforehand. "Ed, I think it will only take us three days, round-trip. If I ask your boss and he says it's okay—and I cover what you would've been paid—will you at least consider it? I really don't want to lose my Bus, Ed, and I can't think of another way." (I figure by using his real name I'll touch his heart, and impress upon him just how important this is to me.)

"Look, even if you *could* pull that off with my boss, Opters, my truck's way overdue for a major tune-up. I *can't* be taking any long drives with it like it is. It's just not gonna work out."

Yes! ... One more hurdle.

"Okay," *Lean forward, maintain full eye contact, speak quietly and deliberately.* "I get it. ... Just let me ask you this: If I *had* been able to get your boss to say it was okay, *and* I paid you for the time you missed, *and* I paid for a major tune-up on your truck, *and* I covered every last penny of anything else that came up. ... If I *had* done *all* of those things, Ed, please, tell me, is there *any other reason* you can think of that would've stopped you from helping me?" (Sales 101: "Closing the deal.")

Perro smiled, closed his eyes, and shook his head, recognizing he'd just lost the argument. A last gasp, he injected a final caveat: "Opters, if you can pull off all of those things you just said—and I mean 100 percent done by tomorrow morning—I can't fucking believe I'm saying this—I'll do it. I'll help you. I'll tow your Bus back."

Yeeessss! Should I feel bad about this? Deep down, he really wanted to help me. Right? He just needed a little nudge to realize it. Right?

Perro didn't know it at the time, but I'd already spoken with his boss and explained the situation. I only needed to call him back and confirm that we were leaving in the morning. We had his truck in a Tuneup Masters' service bay half an hour later.

Yeeessss!

Together we decided it would be simpler (not to mention, a lot safer), if we bypassed Tijuana and Mexicali, and delayed entering Mexico as long as we could. Though it would add nearly a hundred miles to the already nine-hundred-mile trip, we went by way of Tucson, Arizona, before turning south and crossing the border at Nogales, thereby avoiding about four hundred miles of Mexican highway.

It felt strange to be in Mexico again, like I needed to keep my guard up; stay on my toes; be ready. For what, I didn't know. But there's no sugarcoating it: I was strung out and on edge.

"Relax, Opters. There's nothing to worry about. Remember? I'm Mexican. We'll be fine."

He was right; I really should relax. Just having him along was going to make a big difference getting in and out of places. No worries over if: We were heading in the right direction, ordering the right food, paying the right price, or spending the night in a safe place. My best friend was with me—an honest-to-goodness, larger-than-life, card-carrying Mexican—and, *he* was someone I could trust with my life.

My dad had never liked Mexicans, and he did a piss-poor job of keeping that little pique to himself. I have no idea why he didn't like them. He just didn't. Maybe something from his childhood, or inherited from his longshoreman father; he'd never let on. I'd always thought it peculiar, given his deep-seated bigotry toward Mexicans, that he'd moved our family to San Ysidro, of all places—a border town, not a mile north of Tijuana—for the last three of my elementary school years. Most of my classmates lived in Mexico and crossed the border every day to attend. (Counting the one black kid, my sisters, and me, the number of non-Mexicans enrolled in that 300 pupil school never exceeded *four*.)

Perhaps a drop of my dad's venom had contaminated me somewhere along the line, and this was what subconsciously kept me wary of people's motives down here.

"Don't trust 'em. They'll rob you blind if you give 'em half a chance," he'd once coached me.

But none of that lined up with a single soul that I'd come into contact with. Without exception, and every step of the way—from the blackout in the café that first morning, to the old couple who retrieved the camera from the river—to a person they had been, in a word, saints.

I guess Moose had actually nailed it that one night around the fire, when he was (as he used to say) "ed-u-ma-cāting" me about the true character of the Mexican people. Looking back, I suppose it made a lot more sense than I gave him credit for at the time. He believed, because most of the people had so little in the way of material possessions they could call their own, their wealth rested in their intangibles: Honor, family, faith, and generosity. To err with any of these, meant losing it. And for many, these were all they had.

Water skiing on a puddle

If I'd heard it once, I'd heard it a thousand times. "Sure, it's hot in Arizona, but it's a dry heat." (Originally coined as a catchy slogan, I suppose, it rang true.) However, "Oppressively hot; yet dry enough to make your boogers bloody" would work just as well. Thing is, that same heat saddles you for another two thousand miles into Mexico—while the humidity reaches ever more hellish levels, a product of the oceans to either side of you.

Air-conditioning was a luxury upgrade that Perro hadn't gone for when he bought his truck. He said there was no need for it, living by the beach in Southern California. He was adept at quickly putting an end to any grief we gave him for it. "That shit's for princesses and pussies. Besides, it ruins your gas mileage." His truck only got seven miles a gallon as it was; I couldn't imagine it would've made much of a difference.

Rather than waste money on air-conditioning, he'd insisted on the "Sport Package," which included a larger (22.5-gallon) fuel tank, giving us two to three hours, or 150 miles—whichever came first—between fill-ups. And it was probably going to be more often, once we'd hitched my Bus to the back. This was going to cost me a helluva lot more gas money than I'd anticipated.

Paul Wilson

Perro behind the wheel of his truck, basking in the glorious heat and humidity of northern Mexico.

We figured a good goal was for us to make it to Hermosillo, where we'd spend our first night. The second day would be Hermosillo-to-Guasave, hook up the 1DRBUS, and get back to Hermosillo again by dark. Return to Imperial Beach on day three to complete our mission. If everything went right, we'd be on the road about ten to twelve hours each day. Of course, everything rested squarely upon if—and/or how long it took—to find my Bus in Guasave.

Other than the nuisance value of having to stop and fill the gas tank every two hours, our San

Diego-Tucson-Nogales-Hermosillo journey came off without a hitch. Perro and I hadn't brought a tent, figuring we'd just sack out in the back of his truck. For me, it wasn't an issue; after all, I'd ridden nine hundred miles (confined to a fraction of that space) in the back of an old chicken truck just last week. This was a piece of cake. The primary difference being—in the chicken truck, we hadn't had to contend with mosquitos, since we always had a speed-limit-velocity breeze to keep them at bay. Not so, in Perro's truck. Before we'd even unrolled our mats, we stretched two layers of mosquito netting from fender to fender over the bed of his truck. By sundown, it was like watching a low-budget horror film, with the frenetic carpet of hungry mosquitos on the other side of the net. Thousands of little Draculas, every one of them straining to reach you with their tiny syringe. Fresh meat; and not of the equine, bovine, or canine variety. Breed the little bastards with sharks and you could rule the world!

Thankfully, they failed to penetrate our defenses overnight. We'd relieved ourselves into an empty water jug, rather than take the chance of lifting our shroud to pee. Those ratty old, army-surplus mosquito nets were things of beauty. We stayed hidden under them until the morning sun had sent the flock packing.

Our first fill-up of the day was about ninety miles down the road, in a little coastal town called Guaymas. We came upon a circus-like scene on our way back to the highway. Local entrepreneurs had created a one-of-a-kind way to beat the heat (and have some fun while doing it!) At first, we guessed it might be a Saturday morning bullfight the three-deep crowd had encircled—and that thought held—right up until the first Shamu-caliber wave erupted from the arena, dousing everyone!

A brilliant mind obviously had met an industrious spirit. They'd constructed a gargantuan above-ground swimming pool, but one where swimming was not allowed. Leaving it dead center in the middle of the makeshift pond, they had surrounded the base of a large (and presumably, still energized) utility pole. Tethered to it, an old Jet Ski furiously churned through the water, orbiting the pole. Evidently, that alone didn't make for enough of a splash. Fare-paying daredevils were queued up—waiting their turn to *water ski*—from a rope hitched to the back of the Jet Ski.

It was riotously funny to watch. The crowd taunted each skier, challenging them to veer ever closer, rips of cool spray their reward. The all-too-common wipeouts elicited groans, laughter, booing, and applause, growing louder with each successive crash and burn. We had no idea of how long they'd kept this up today, but most of the water skiers already bore cuts and bruises *before* grabbing the rope and yelling, "¡Ahora!" (Now!)

My powers of persuasion were good, but not sufficient to convince Perro to give it a go ... unless "I tried it first."

Beers with El Chapo

An hour short of our destination, Perro asked me to fill in a few of blanks in the "How the 1DRBUS ended up in Guasave" yarn I'd spun for him.

"Hey, Opters. Jelly said you guys almost ended up in a Mexican jail down here, but wouldn't tell me more about it. How'd that happen?"

A not-so-minor detail, I'd hoped could wait for later.

"Uh, what'd he tell you about it?" *I was thinking we'd all laugh about this when it was over.*

"C'mon, Opters! I need to know what I might be getting into down here. Spill the beans, already!"

I guess I owe him that much. Here goes nothing ...

"Well, remember how I was telling you about having to get a taxi cab to tow us the twenty miles back to Guasave after we broke down, and it was kinda gnarly because they only had a short piece of rope?"

"Yeah, so what have you been leaving out?"

"Uh … well … the Federales chased us. But we got away."

"And …?"

"The taxi had some pot in the trunk."

Perro turned to me, reached up, and lowered his mirror-lensed, Aviator-style sunglasses so he could look me straight in the eyes. "Like how much pot?"

Our right tires found gravel, the truck drifting onto the shoulder.

"Hey! Watch the road and I'll tell you!"

"HOW MUCH, Opters?"

"A trunk full of bricks, at least 150 kilos."

This time intentionally, Perro pulled off the highway onto the shoulder, and skidded his truck to a stop. A cloud of dust trailed us at first, but quickly caught up and enveloped us.

"Do you know where the fuck we are?! No one has that much pot in this part of Mexico unless they are members of the Sinaloa Cartel! So let me get this straight, Opters: You had two guys—members of the Sinaloa Cartel—tow your Bus to Guasave and take it to their ranch for safekeeping, and you expect to just pull up and tell 'em we're here to pick it up?! Are you fucking crazy?!"

I suppose it does sound a little "out there" when you put it that way …

"How was I supposed to know they were in a cartel? I mean, they seemed like good guys, you know, helping us out like that and everything. Maybe just call and talk to them when we get to Guasave and see how they sound, okay? They gave me their phone number. Just to be sure, I got one off their taxi, too. Will you just call and see how it goes? I mean, we've come all this way and everything."

"Okay. Look. This is the one and only way we're going to do this thing. I'll call and tell 'em who we are and why we're here—straight up—the whole truth. If I don't think they sound happy to hear from you, or it seems the least bit sketchy, we're turning 'round and going back to IB, Bus or no Bus. That's how it's gotta be. No other way. Got it?"

No room for negotiating here. I just need to say a prayer and hope for the best.

"Yeah, thanks Perro. Hopefully, this doesn't all end up being a total waste of time. At least we got to watch the water skiers, right?" *If that's the overarching memory of this trip, it's gonna suck ... or will it? I suppose that's a better highlight than being kidnapped and held for ransom by the Sinaloa Cartel ... They wouldn't do that ... Would they?*

"Yeah, let's do it your way."

Guasave was every bit as depressing a place as I remembered from my brief tour last week. Who decides that *this* is the spot to start a town? I mean the landscape is exactly the same wind-blown dirt for miles in every direction, so why here? Even so, our timing must have been better this afternoon; there actually was activity along the main drag. An eclectic assortment of old sedans and farm trucks lined the streets. The sidewalks were monopolized by old men in cowboy hats, and young mothers in their weekend finery, mesh shopping bags in one hand, controlling curious toddlers with the other. We drove past a line of taxis parked in front of the bus station, their drivers taking a collective smoke break.

"Any of those guys look familiar?"

"Nah, neither do any of their cars. Hey, do you want to get something to eat, and call 'em after?" My anxiety level's been sky-high ever since Perro told me about the whole "cartel" thing.

"No, I wanna get this over with and get the fuck outta Guasave, that's what I want."

"There are probably phones in the station." *I'd really rather not see the inside of another one.*

"Stay here with my truck. Some of these guys down here would kill to have one like this." *So, I'm the guy they'd be killing to get it? Thanks, Perro.*

"Okay. Here's the number. Be nice." *Yeah, that sounded stupid to me, too.*

Perro shook his head and walked away mumbling, "Be nice … Ay!"

He was gone for a good five minutes before returning.

"Did you get ahold of 'em?"

"Yeah. They said to meet them at the PEMEX up the street."

"Oh man! That's great! Did everything sound okay?"

Pulling his Aviators lower on his nose again, and looking me in the eyes, "They said it was better if we follow 'em to where your Bus is …"

Probably tricky to find.

"… Because strangers aren't allowed in that part of town without an escort."

Oh.

"I forgot to ask you their names."

"Joaquín and Angel. They're cousins or buddies or something. Joaquín is our age. Moose said his nickname is 'Chapo.' Said it means, 'Shorty,' but not to call him that unless he says it's okay. He's the one in charge."

"I must've been talking with him. He said he had to go get Angel from his aunt's house, and they'd see us in about twenty minutes."

We drove to the designated meeting spot, but decided to wait a bit before pulling in. (No need to raise unnecessary interest by hanging around the PEMEX before we needed to.) When we did, Perro insisted on parking where he could pull out—forward or reverse—"if the situation goes south. ..." Right on time, my taxi friends tucked their white Chevy in alongside us and climbed out. They seemed happy to see *me*, but there was a discernable tension between Joaquín and Perro. I noticed for the first time how relatively small in stature he was, standing next to my 6-foot-2, 180-pound friend. *Or maybe they were a little wary of new faces in this neck of the woods because of their marijuana business?*

Formal introductions completed, we fell in behind the taxi and followed it across town. Joaquín drove; Angel (turned half around) had his eyes fixed on us the whole time.

That's bullshit. He only turned around long enough to pass the joint to Moose before!

Maybe we were making him nervous. Perro had a tendency to tailgate now and then, and this was one of those times.

"I think you're making 'em nervous, following so close, Perro. Besides, I got my fill of that view last week."

"I don't want to lose 'em. Who knows where the fuck they're taking us, and I sure as shit don't want to get lost and wander into some kind of cartel hell out here."

Good point.

At most, two car lengths behind them, we turned onto a long, straight, narrow lane, tightly strung barbwire fencing hemming us in on both sides. No chance of a wrong turn now. About a half mile in, we came to a guard shack, complete with the type of swing-arm barricade you see at railroad crossings stateside. No "Double Rs," ringing bells, and flashing red lights here, though. Just two guys in ranch-hand attire, one of them with an AK-47 at the ready, cradling it against his chest.

"Goddammit, Opters! I told you this was stupid. Now what're we supposed to do?"

"Fuck it, Perro. Follow 'em in. It's not like we can back out now."

Wow. When they'd said they'd keep my Bus safe ...

After a brief conversation between Joaquín and the two guards, the barricade lifted and we were allowed to pass. We stayed close to him for another quarter of a mile or so before the taxi came to a stop in front of us. Joaquín got out, leaving his door swung wide open, walked back to us, said something to Perro in Spanish, and returned to his car.

"What'd he say?"

"He said not to lag or stray in here. His boss won't like it."

"Anything else?"

"Yeah. No pictures."

"Got it."

For all of the security and hullabaloo of getting in there, once inside it looked pretty much like any other produce packinghouse operation we'd seen (well, maybe except this one was in a clearing, cut into the middle of a grove of trees). Along one side was a long, two-story, windowless, corrugated tin warehouse, with several stake-bed farm trucks at one end and a long-haul semi-truck backed up to the other. A large engine, in what appeared to be the front end of an old bus that had been reduced to a mere chunk of chassis, rumbled fitfully, ingeniously modified to spin an equally jerry-rigged generator. Two men guided a third, maneuvering a newly minted, bright-orange-and-black Toyota forklift, adding another stack of empty pallets to an already impressive inventory. A warehouse or barracks of some sort, surrounded by smaller outbuildings, dominated the far side of the main yard. Straight ahead, a row of cars and pickup trucks lined a fence, and at the far end was parked ... the 1DRBUS!

"It's here! Perro, look! It's here!"

"That's fucking great, Opters. Let's hope they let us leave with it … and my truck."

We followed the taxi through the yard to where the Bus was and pulled alongside them. I had my door halfway open before Perro stopped me.

"Hey, let's stay put until they tell us to get out, okay?"

C'mon, Perro! You're treating this like a fucking hostage exchange. Lighten up already!

"Whatever you say," pulling my door back closed until it clicked, engaging the latch.

Angel stayed with the Chevy while Joaquín walked over, climbed up on the running board below my door, stuck his head in the window, and broke into a big smile.

"Aquí está, amigo mío. Nadie la ha tocado. La hemos mantenido a salvo para usted como lo prometimos."

"Shake the man's hand, Opters."

"What'd he say?"

"Shake his hand already! He said: Here it is, and they haven't let anyone touch it."

Joaquín hopped down and backed up a few paces. I finished opening my door, turned, jumped down from the truck, and went to him with my hand extended, an irrepressible grin on my face.

"¡Gracias! ¡Muchas gracias, mi amigo!"

"De nada. Te hicimos una promesa."

"What'd he say?"

"He said they made a promise to you."

Wow.

I was still gripping and shaking Joaquín's hand when Angel joined us, so I let go and turned my attention to him.

"¡Muchas gracias, Angel!"

"De nada, mi amigo."

I got behind the wheel and the guys pushed the 1DRBUS back so we could hook it up to the truck for towing. I turned my head and looked around the back long enough to see that, indeed, nothing had been touched. Everything (including all of our still-encased-in-mud gear) was exactly as we'd left it. I had Perro ask them if they could make an exception to the "no pictures" rule, so I could get one of them in front of my Bus. They agreed, as long as we pointed the camera so it only showed jungle in the photo behind them. Concerned we'd be stopped, I snapped a quick shot, but before allowing me to take a second, Joaquín insisted on climbing onto the back of the truck, where he could sit on the raised tailgate—to avoid looking so short next to Perro.

Afterward, they helped us get all hitched up for the long drive home. We were to follow them out, but *only* until we reached the main drag, making it clear we'd be on our own from there. (They didn't want to chance being seen with us near the highway, just in case the Federales who chased us were around today.)

Shit. I hadn't thought of that. I hope they don't see us later, put two and two together, and pull me and Perro over! Oh well, at least we won't have a trunk full of marijuana to worry about.

Time to hit the road, I asked Perro how much I should offer to pay them for storing my Bus, keeping it safe, and everything. (I came prepared to give them a hundred dollars.)

"Mi amigo quiere saber cuánto pagarte." ("My friend wants to know how much to pay you.")

Angel deferred to Joaquín. "No hicimos esto para obtener dinero; te ayudamos porque estaba bien. Aunque tengo un poco de sed. No rechazaríamos algunas cervezas." ("We didn't do this to get money; we helped you because it was right. I *am* a little thirsty though. We wouldn't refuse some beers.")

Perro laughed and turned to me. "They said there was no need to pay them anything, but you better be sure to bonus me out when we get home. They said they'd be stoked if you bought them some beers."

The "bonus me out" part went right over my head, but I had Perro assure them plenty of cervezas were most definitely in their immediate future. We left the compound and followed them into town, stopping at a little market on the outskirts. Joaquín stayed outside with Perro, and Angel came with me into the store. There were only two kinds of beer, so with Angel's blessing, I bought two cases of "Modelo Especial," in stubby little bottles; a beer I'd seen in cans, but never in bottles shaped like that.

Paul Wilson

Our Guasave "parcel delivery service" crew,
left to right: Angel, Joaquín, Perro, and some guy photobombing us.

After we'd each downed a few cold ones (the four of us sitting in the back of Perro's truck in the *mercado* parking lot), the conversation began to get much more comfortable and flowed freely between us—Perro serving as interpreter. Angel didn't say much, but Joaquín was full of questions. He asked our real names, and was curious about how we got our nicknames. In turn, he gave us the okay to call him by his nickname, "Chapo," noting that only his family and good friends were allowed to call him that. Turned out that Joaquín (April), Perro (September), and I (January) shared 1957 as our birth year, and had being age twenty-one in common. The three of us revealed to each other how—from a very young age—our fathers had insisted we work long hours for them: Joaquín in the fields harvesting poppies and marijuana, me in my dad's cabinet shop, and Perro picking fruit. All three of our fathers had been devoid of compassion and quick to dish out physical punishments. And each of our mothers had done their best to provide us a moral underpinning, rooted in a belief in God. Joaquín said his dad was *un maldito borracho* ("a mean drunk"), while Perro's and mine didn't require any lubrication; their nastiness came naturally. This got me thinking about how radically different the cultural circumstances of our formative years had been, yet how uncannily similar our foundational challenges were. The three of us shared a common bond—and a common mission: Our earliest memories were of tyrannical fathers, benevolent mothers, and of being "dirt floor poor." To a man, we were hell-bent on proving our dads had underestimated us—and making our mothers proud.

We talked and drank for a long time. It was the mosquitos' arrival near dusk that provided the impetus for us to say our goodbyes and get on the road home. I found myself liking Joaquín, and thought of him as a friend (but not one that I pictured spending much time with after today). He had stepped up and helped us that memorable day a week ago when we needed it the most, taking a real risk to do so. He'd been true to his word and kept the 1DRBUS safe for me, when it probably would have been easier (and definitely more profitable) to have stripped it, sold it, or just kept it hidden until I gave up looking. So what if he had a little drug business going? He was a solid guy.

I prayed this wasn't just "wishful thinking" on Perro's part.

A marked man

"Man. What a trip, eh?"

"Yeah, I know. Can you believe where they had my Bus?"

"Fuck your Bus. Did you see the AK-47 that guy had? There was probably another in the guard shack for his buddy, and enough for an army in one of those buildings."

"It's kinda weird that drug runners would make it their duty to keep my Bus safe, eh?"

"Not really. Joaquín told me that in Sinaloa, providing drugs to the States is considered more of a business than a crime. Ripping someone off showed you lacked honor ... and, in *his* business, a lack of honor would get you killed."

"Oh."

We'd gotten out of town much later than we'd planned to, and it was rapidly getting dark. We hadn't thought to bring anything along to link the Bus taillights to the truck, and decided it was smarter to spend the night in Guaymas and park near the water-skiing pond from earlier that morning. Still enjoying the adrenaline buzz of our visit to the smugglers' compound (not to mention, having a long afternoon's worth of beers under our belts), we picked up a couple more six packs of Modelo to celebrate our success, and wind down a bit.

The mosquitos the night before in Hermosillo had nothing on the ones ruling over Guaymas. We stretched the two nets over the truck's fenders like before, took shelter, and got busy drinking our beers. Our mission was far from over, but we pounded down cervezas like we'd just won the World Series. I don't remember falling asleep, but I do have a foggy recollection of partially waking in the middle of the night from a vivid nightmare, one where a vicious storm was drenching us in sizzling-hot rain drops.

Perro was the first to awaken the next morning.

"Opters! Oh my God, Opters! Your arms! Your back! Oh shit, your face! Oh my God!"

I'd snagged the mosquito netting somehow during the night and pulled it free from the fender on my side of the truck. It'd dipped low enough to allow the little bastards to reach me through the mesh and start an impromptu rave. I must have felt it and flailed around, trying to rehang the net. Whether I was at all successful or not remains unknown. In the morning, the net was wrapped around both arms, laying against one side of my face, and stretched tightly across my bare back from shoulders to waist. With the exception of three intersecting wrinkles in the netting on one shoulder (that'd kept their "weapons of mosquito suction" at bay), a bright red mosaic of bites covered me. I can only compare the feeling to being scalded with hot water—with no interruption forthcoming—and unbearably itchy. My skin was on fire, and there was nothing available to extinguish it.

"Opters, you gotta look at this."

Thanks Perro, I can feel it. I don't need to see it.

"I'm on fire! Can you die from this? I mean how many bites before they've sucked all your blood?"

"You gotta see it. Look at your back in my side mirror, especially the back of your shoulder. They signed their work."

Fucking little assassins.

I managed to see most of the patch of bite-free skin by looking over my shoulder, but climbed down from the truck bed to use the side mirror anyway, mostly to satisfy Perro. The three intersecting furrows that had denied their hypodermic feeding tubes—when viewed in a mirror—had left a near-perfect, eight-inch-tall, capital letter "K" of unblemished skin, silhouetted against a field of a thousand angry mosquito bites.

"You've been through enough"

The lady at the local farmacia was visibly alarmed when she looked at my back, but could offer only condolences, and some non-prescription ointment to apply to it. The cream didn't help with the itching at all, but did accent the bloodsuckers' masterpiece with a gentle pink hue. Getting comfortable was impossible. As if the 110-degree heat and the 99 percent humidity weren't enough, I had uncountable legions of demonic bumps to contend with.

Staying overnight in Guaymas instead of Hermosillo had already put us several hours behind schedule, and my "Saturday Net Fever" held us up even more. Not about to catch a break, we hit one construction delay after another all day long (several requiring us to sit in traffic—in the sun—for an hour or more before proceeding). It became a given we would run out of daylight before reaching the border at Nogales, so we decided to take a shortcut and enter via "Lukeville, Arizona." Our reasoning also took into account this route would get us off the main highway, and reduce our chances of being hassled by the Federales for not having working lights on the Bus.

We finally pulled into the town on the Mexican side of the Lukeville crossing a little after midnight. It was called Hombres Blancos, which translates literally to "White Men." (I wondered why they decided to call it that. Maybe because it was the last place in the world you would expect to find white men?) We followed our map to the border—only to find it closed, a sign on the closed gate saying it would reopen at 4 a.m. Too worn out and road weary to go anywhere else at this hour, we pulled up as far as we could, turned off the engine, and sat there.

"At least we'll be first in line when they open."

I didn't get as much as a glance in my direction in response.

We must've dozed off, because an obnoxiously bright flashlight beam startled us into consciousness sometime later, the gate blocking the lane in front of us having been rolled aside already. We were still first in line. In fact, we remained the only ones in line. Reclaiming his bearings, Perro fired up his truck, pulled forward slowly, and stopped when the U.S. border officer raised his hand. He looked us up and down before approaching Perro's window.

"What part of Mexico are you two coming from this morning?" He shone his light in my direction first, so I answered, "Guasave, in Sinaloa."

Ah shit. Why didn't I just tell him about the cartel compound we hung out at yesterday? My brain ...

"Oh yeah? Whose VW is that?"

"It's mine, sir. We had some problems and had to tow it back." Unconsciously, I rubbed the side of my face with my left hand.

"What's that all over your arm and face?"

"Mosquito bites, sir. The net came loose and fell on me while I was asleep last night."

"Hmmm."

Evidently finished with me for now, the officer focused his light on Perro briefly, before stepping back a few feet.

Oh man, this must be where he tells us to step out of the truck, and summons someone to escort us inside, where we'll be subjected to a full-blown, body-cavity-invading, search.

He ran the flashlight's beam down the length of the truck, stopping when he reached the front of my Bus. He walked back to it and shined his light, first through the windshield and then, one by one, into each side window, before turning it off and returning to the truck. Reaching Perro's door, he clicked his flashlight on (aiming it at my Bus), focused the beam on us for a second, and then back to the Bus again. Clicking it off, he looked at the two of us, shook his head, and said,

"Go on. You've been through enough."

EPILOGUE

Steve Warren, aka Jelly:

Jelly and Moose grew distant after we got back. However, he patched things up with Sherri and they had a son together. They moved from The Manor and got a place of their own. Tragically, Sherri died in her sleep one night while Jelly was away on a six-month hitch, working in a Humboldt, California marijuana-processing operation with some fellow Manorites.

Later, Jelly started an exotic palm tree business at his parents' house, but shut it down after one of the trees fell during a windstorm and hit him in the face, injuring him badly. It was a lengthy recovery that included facial reconstruction surgery, and he never was quite the same afterward. He became something of a hermit, rarely leaving home or dating, choosing instead to make his living as an online gambler. He never returned to La Ticla.

We all "pitched in" when it came time for Jelly
to move out of The Manor.

Ed Moss, aka Moose:

Jeez, where do I start? Successfully evading arrest stateside
after our return, Moose soon headed back south, reconnected
with our Guasave friends, Joaquín and Angel, and began
transporting drugs north for them via Baja. After several
successful runs (and tipping the ship's crew off because he
was unable to wait out the 14 hour crossing without smoking
a doobie) the Federales became suspicious of his grossly
overweight surfboard travel bags and busted him departing
the ferry in Cabo San Lucas. He spent some time in a La Paz
jail before being transferred to Tijuana, at which time he was

handed over to the U.S. judicial system and incarcerated in Chuckawalla Valley State Prison in Blythe, California, for his earlier manslaughter conviction.

Upon parole, Moose collaborated with Joaquín to help assemble a high-volume smuggling ring that ran untold thousands of pounds of drugs through Imperial Beach, California, filling the void left when the famed "Coronado Company" went down in the early eighties. At great risk, they circumvented the more established "Tijuana Cartel" and helped the Guasave-Sinaloa Cartel gain entrance into the lucrative Tijuana-San Diego smuggling corridor. The night the Imperial Beach faction of the ring was busted (via an undercover DEA agent who'd infiltrated,) Moose initially escaped capture, but was arrested and arraigned for his involvement a few months later. He skipped out on bail, embarking on another long surf trip to La Ticla (this time with Perro and two others) and then stayed behind to be with a Mexican girl he'd fallen in love with. By then, the secret of La Ticla had gone viral—attracting throngs of surfers from Texas to New Zealand—and had Moose established a tidy little business supplying the visitors with local herb, purchased from the "La Familia Michoacana/ Knights Templar" cartel in the Ostula Valley region to the east of La Ticla.

One morning, he made the triple error of: rejecting a load of marijuana as inferior, revealing he had a significant amount of cash on hand, and letting other surfers know he considered the pot bunk. Offending the cartel lieutenant proved a fatal mistake. An ambush was set up on the road leaving La Ticla, one Moose recognized and nearly evaded, before falling victim to a lucky shot, when a bullet passed through the trunk of his car and struck him mid-back. He bled out and died on the way to the nearest hospital, in Tecomán. His ashes later were scattered into the surf at his favorite slice of paradise, La Ticla.

Paul Wilson

Stoned off his ass and thinking it a good idea to ride one,
Moose matched wits with this burro outside our camp
one afternoon, and lost. It never budged an inch.

Ed Leon, aka Perro:

Coincidentally, Perro was on a coffee break from his job
at the lumberyard the morning the PSA jet collided with
a small plane over San Diego and crashed, taking 144 lives.
He'd watched the whole thing from atop a stack of plywood.
Going to La Ticla had become something of a rite of passage
for residents of The Manor, and, a few years later, Perro
spent three months there with Moose and another longtime
Manorite, Oscar "Tongs" Andrade, and Oscar's buddy, Dave
"The Statue" Pardee.

Perro never really outgrew being a kid. I mean that in all of
the best ways. He knows how to have fun and enjoy life, but
keeps his family and friendships number one at all times. He's

been rewarded with five adult children and several grandkids who cherish him.

Perro and I remain close to this day. He will always be my best friend. "My brother from another mother."

Mr. Aubel's seventh-grade woodshop class, circa 1969.
That's Perro at the back of the line to the water fountain—about to plunk the guy taking a drink with a chunk of wood
"Because he was taking too long."

The Author, aka Opters:

It took a lot longer than it should have, but I eventually got my shit together and took to heart the many lessons of those five and a half memorable weeks. I continued to live in The Manor for another four years before moving out to get married and raise a family.

My mom served as my rock until 1987, when she succumbed to a multi-year battle with multiple myeloma (her body riddled with tumors that devoured her skeleton—claiming a hundred fractures in all—one at a time.) My dad's speaker-cabinet business reached remarkable levels of success, affording him a mansion and a fancy boat moored at his private dock on San Diego Bay. He loved European sports cars, and skipped my mom's funeral to test-drive the latest model, remaining an asshole to the bitter end. He died while checking the contents of his safe-deposit boxes at the bank, and willed his entire estate to the Salvation Army. When I was a teenager, he'd often lamented that he expected me to grace a "Ten Most Wanted" poster one day, or end up living under a pier. He was close, I suppose. Seven or eight poster-size enlargements of photographs I've taken adorn the lobby walls of our local post office, and I have an amazing view of Crystal Pier in San Diego from my home.

Twice married (with Perro serving as my Best Man both times), I've been blessed with two amazing (now adult) children, their spouses, and five equally special grandkids. The closest I've come to returning to La Ticla is looking at it on a map.

My favorite pastime these days.

Joaquín, aka El Chapo:

Notorious as the birthplace and headquarters of the Guasave–Sinaloa Cartel (headed by Joaquín "El Chapo" Guzman from the early 1980s through 2016), Guasave frequently is in the news for all of the wrong reasons. In 2017, our DEA declared that the cartel remains the largest importer of marijuana, cocaine (in excess of five hundred tons), and heroin into the United States; and the top manufacturer of methamphetamine and Ecstasy in the world. It wasn't until I saw his booking photo years later that I knew for certain that our Guasave friend, Joaquín "El Chapo" Guzman, had gone on to become much more than "Moose's Sinaloa cartel connection."

Joaquín, age twenty-one in 1978.   Joaquín, age thirty-six in 1993.

1DRBUS, aka The Wonderbus:

My Bus was never quite the same after Mexico. I spent hundreds of hours spiffing it up again, and drove it another two years—until two friends each lost a leg, while behind the wheel of an old Splittie like mine in separate accidents. (It was common practice to rest your left foot on the back of the driver's side headlight in those days, and a simple fender bender could take that leg off at the knee.) I sold the 1DRBUS at a local swap meet. I don't recall whether or not I ever told the buyers to avoid using the defroster, because it was still blowing sand.

"Faster than a speeding bullet! More powerful than a locomotive!" Unfortunately, it couldn't swim.

The Manor:

Although The Manor was situated across the street from the beach, it was not unheard of for a rogue wave to strike the building. This particular one strong-armed our famously "thrifty" owner into installing new flooring in each of the ground-level apartments.

La Ticla:

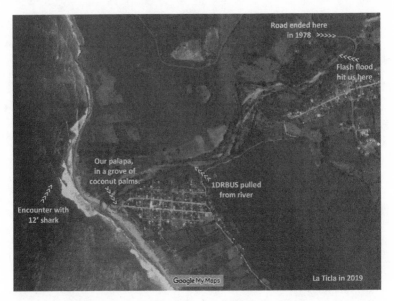

As we feared, once the bridge was completed, La Ticla was changed forever. What had been a sleepy little village of six or eight huts is now a bustling town, complete with traffic signals, restaurants and beachfront hotels. *Our* surf break is never empty.

ACKNOWLEDGEMENTS

My best friend, Ed, aka Perro: He's saved my life more times than would fit into this book. Ed patiently read my rough drafts, and helped fill in the blanks of a few fuzzy spots in my recollections.

My daughter, Lindsey: She's heard most of the stories in this book a hundred times over, and loves me anyway. Lindsey was my sounding board throughout. Without her help, this book would've never exited the cul-de-sac it was circling.

Barbara Noe Kennedy: She is undoubtedly the best editor I could have possibly found for my work. Barbara demonstrated an amazing eye for detail, and a studied insight into everything, large and small, and where my manuscript had missed the mark. Above all, she maintained the unwavering patience necessary to deal with someone who hadn't written more than a grocery list since the ninth grade.

Derek Murphy: Without the incredible depth of knowledge he imparts via his online tutorials, I'd still be unfocused and unsure of the steps necessary to make this a book. Derek personally worked his magic on the cover design, and I couldn't be happier with the results.

The San Diego Fire Department: They extinguished a full-blown structure fire in an apartment below mine last year, before it could consume our building. Losing my place to live was of secondary concern to me. Tucked away in my attic was the carton full of forty-year-old notes, records and photographs that went into the telling of this story. Without them, not many people would believe all of this had really happened.

God: I hesitated for many years to tell this story publicly, largely because I was ashamed of the crappy things I'd done, and it couldn't be told properly without them. Through prayer—and the confidence that age and experience bestow—I came to accept that by sharing it, warts and all, someone else might realize it's never too late to change your life's direction. Our Heavenly Father is beyond patient with our faults, and loves us unconditionally. I give thanks to Him every day for the miracles, the incredible riches of people, experiences, and forgiveness He has shown me. Thank you, God. (Now before you think I'm getting all preachy on you, I understand that my God may not be the same as your God. That's okay. I'm pretty sure they're pals.)

Made in the USA
Coppell, TX
05 October 2023

22472370R00157